12th Edition

W9-ARQ-960

The National Anti-Vivisection Society

PERSONAL CARE FOR PEOPLE WHO CARE

A guide to using your purchasing power as a consumer
to help end the cruel and wasteful practice of testing cosmetics,
personal care and companion animal products on animals.

A publication of the National Anti-Vivisection Society

Animal Advocates for Humane Science

Personal Care for People Who Care

Personal Care for People Who Care is a publication of the National Anti-Vivisection Society (NAVS), a not-for-profit organization dedicated to abolishing the exploitation of animals used in research, education and product testing. NAVS promotes greater compassion, respect and justice for animals through educational programs based on respected ethical and scientific theory and supported by extensive documentation of the cruelty and waste of vivisection. NAVS' educational programs are directed at increasing public awareness about vivisection, identifying humane solutions to human problems, developing alternatives to the use of animals and working with like-minded individuals and groups to effect changes which help to end the suffering inflicted on innocent animals.

For more information about NAVS and our educational and advocacy programs, please turn to page 192.

The information provided in this book is based on the most current data available at the time of publication. For the most up-to-date information, visit the NAVS website at www.navs.org or contact the company directly.

The National Anti-Vivisection Society
53 W. Jackson Blvd., Suite 1552
Chicago, IL 60604
(800) 888-NAVS (6287)
Fax: (312) 427-6524

Visit us at www.navs.org
Email: navs@navs.org

TABLE OF CONTENTS

Introduction: Learn How You Have the Power to Make a Difference

Choose to Shop Cruelty Free!	6
How to Make the Most of This Book	8
How the Main Directory Is Put Together	10
How Animals Are Used in Product Testing	12
Why Testing Products on Animals Doesn't Work	14
The Smart—and Humane—Solution to Animal Testing	16
Why Companies Still Test on Animals	18
Decoding the Language of Animal Testing Policies	20

Main Directory: Use Your Purchasing Power to Make a Difference

Directory of Cruelty-Free Products by Product Type	26
How to Use the Main Directory	36
Directory of Companies That DO and DO NOT Test on Animals	38

Appendices: Pursuing the Cruelty-Free Way of Living

Parent Companies Behind Product Names	138
Cruelty-Free Mail Order Companies	148
Animal-Derived Ingredients Used in Consumer Products	154
Health-Based Charities That DO and DO NOT Fund Animal Research	156
Frequently Asked Questions and Answers About Animal Testing	184

About the Publisher and Discovering More Ways to Help Animals

Making a Difference for Animals	190
About NAVS	192
NAVS Membership Application	195

Learn How You

Choose to Shop Cruelty Free! 6

How to Make the Most of This Book 8

How the Main Directory Is Put Together 10

How Animals Are Used in Product Testing 12

Why Testing Products on Animals Doesn't Work 14

The Smart—and Humane—Solution
to Animal Testing 16

Why Companies Still Test on Animals 18

Decoding the Language of Animal Testing Policies 20

Have the Power to Make a Difference

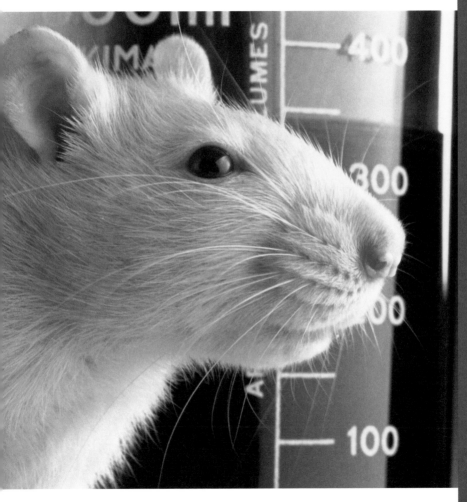

CHOOSE TO SHOP CRUELTY FREE!

This handy, take-along guide makes it simple and convenient.

Have you ever thought about how the everyday products you shop for are determined to be safe for you and your family? The grim fact is that all too many companies safety test their products on live animals as part of the long and complex process of developing new and "improved" cosmetics, personal care items and household products. These tests cause extreme pain and suffering to the animals involved.

Unbelievable as it may seem that in the 21st century cosmetic companies are still harming animals to test mascara, it is even more appalling that companies are not required to do it! That's right—there are no federal regulations mandating cosmetic companies to test their final products, or the ingredients used to make them, on animals.

For more information on government regulations regarding animal testing, see page 18.

What's more, there is abundant evidence that these tests are not only inhumane, they are also scientifically flawed. There are many ways of testing the safety of consumer products without using animals.

For these reasons, many animal advocates have joined the National Anti-Vivisection Society in opposing the use of animals in product testing. One important way we have of demonstrating our beliefs is to shop "cruelty free," and all that means is choosing products that have not been animal-tested. The term "cruelty free" refers to the product testing policy of a company that does not use animals in testing either its ingredients or final products.

Personal Care for People Who Care is your guide to identifying those products that are and aren't tested on animals, so you can make the choice to speak up for animals every time you shop.

By choosing products that have not been tested on animals, you're demonstrating your compassion while supporting those companies that opt not to test on animals. You're also making a strong statement to those companies that continue to test on animals.

You may not think that one person buying one bottle of shampoo can make a difference—but that's just not so. Companies *do* respond to consumer pressure. In fact, it was during the 1980s, when committed individuals, just like you, worked together to put the pressure on Revlon to stop testing on animals. And once Revlon stopped testing on animals, many major companies followed.

You *can* make a difference, and together we can bring about real and positive change for animals.

So have a heart for animals, and shop cruelty free! We hope this new edition of *Personal Care for People Who Care* helps.

Why we call ourselves the National Anti-Vivisection Society.

The word "vivisection" refers to the act of cutting into, dissecting or harming the body of an animal, especially for the purpose of product testing, biomedical research and education. Vivisection is also called animal experimentation. The National Anti-Vivisection Society opposes this practice on both ethical and scientific grounds.

To learn more about how vivisection harms animals and people, and how you can help put an end to this cruel and wasteful practice, please visit our website at www.navs.org.

HOW TO MAKE THE MOST OF THIS BOOK

The main part of this book—the alphabetical directory of companies and product names that do and do not test on animals—begins on page 38. Right before that, on page 26, begins the section listing Cruelty-Free Products by Product Type, such as "hair care" and "laundry products."

On page 36, you'll find an explanation of the symbols we've assigned to each entry based solely on the information the company gave us. The same explanation of the symbols also appears on the back flap, which you can use as a placeholder when you take *Personal Care for People Who Care* shopping with you.

But don't stop there—there's much more to this guide than the directory. In the next several pages, you'll learn why we believe it's cruel and wasteful to test products on animals. You'll also discover why companies continue to test on animals,

even though there is abundant evidence to prove that it is scientifically unsound.

In the pages following the directory, we've provided a number of listings that will be helpful as you explore the cruelty-free lifestyle. These include:

- **Parent Companies Behind Product Names** *(Begins on page 138)*

  With so many companies and their subsidiaries, divisions and product names, it can be confusing to figure out who owns what! This section helps you identify major parent companies whose names may not be readily identifiable with their products.

- **Cruelty-Free Mail Order Companies** *(Begins on page 148)*

  This is a quick reference for those who can't find cruelty-free products locally…or who simply enjoy the convenience of ordering online, by telephone or by mail.

- **Animal-Derived Ingredients Used in Consumer Products** *(Begins on page 154)*

  If you'd like to avoid products that contain animal by-products, this section is for you.

- **Health-Based Charities That DO and DO NOT Fund Animal Research** *(Begins on page 156)*

  Animal advocates who also oppose using animals in biomedical research will find this section to be helpful when deciding which not-for-profit organizations to support.

How the Main Directory Is Put Together

Personal Care for People Who Care is the result of months of research by NAVS staff members, who tabulate the results of the surveys we send to hundreds of companies across the country.

Our main directory includes listings of companies that do and do not test their products and/or ingredients on animals; it is intended to be used for informational purposes only. Being included in *Personal Care for People Who Care* does not imply any endorsement of a company's products by the National Anti-Vivisection Society, nor do we take orders for any products identified in the listings. For more information on purchasing products, please contact the company directly.

We have made every effort to include as many companies as possible, and to provide as much information as possible. Company policies can and do change, so if you'd like to keep your book as up-to-date as possible, please visit our website at www.navs.org.

If you contact a company directly and obtain information that you feel would be useful to fellow compassionate shoppers, we would greatly appreciate your sending it along to us at **pcfeedback@navs.org,** so that we can immediately update our online database. Also, if you know of a company that is not listed in this book, please let us know via email at **pcfeedback@navs.org,** and we'll do our best to find out about it.

If you would like to contact companies directly about their testing policies, we've made it easy for you by providing a telephone number and website (if they've been provided to us) in each company's listing in the main directory. That way, you can visit the company website and contact them by clicking on "Contact Us."

What you WON'T find in this book.

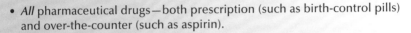

Current government regulations specifically require companies that manufacture certain products to safety test on animals before releasing them to the market. These include:

- *All* pharmaceutical drugs—both prescription (such as birth-control pills) and over-the-counter (such as aspirin).

- *All* cosmetics and personal care products that are also intended to treat or prevent disease, or that affect the structure or functions of the human body, such as:
  – Suntan preparations intended to protect against sunburn
  – Deodorants that are also antiperspirants
  – Anti-dandruff shampoos
  – Topical acne medications

You will, however, find a few suntan preparations, antiperspirants, anti-dandruff shampoos and topical acne medications in this book. These products either contain ingredients that were animal-tested years ago and are no longer tested on animals **or** are products made from naturally derived ingredients only.

We have not included vitamins in this book as our concentration is solely on cosmetics, personal care, household and companion animal products. The government does not currently require companies to test vitamins on animals. Animal testing of vitamins would only be required if the vitamin was suspected to be a toxic agent.

You will find no generic products in this book. There are so many store brands and generic products on the market that space does not allow us to list them all. Many store brand products are manufactured by companies that produce the same national brands, but not always, and there are some companies that manufacture multiple brands.

HOW ANIMALS ARE USED IN PRODUCT TESTING

Animals suffer severe pain and distress under the guise of public safety.

Despite the cruelty and waste of animal testing, millions of animals are used each year under the false assumption that testing products on live animals protects the public.

Rats, mice, rabbits and guinea pigs are the species most commonly used in outmoded tests that attempt to determine the potential harm a substance can do to a living creature when ingested or inhaled, or otherwise comes into contact with the body. Rabbits are used most extensively in eye irritancy tests because their eyes are large—and the animals themselves, like rodents, are inexpensive, readily available and easy to maintain and handle.

These toxicological tests include eye and skin irritancy tests, as well as tests which determine the internal effects of a substance. The most frequently used animal tests are various versions of the Draize eye and skin irritancy tests, and the LD-50 test. Both of these tests were

designed in the mid-1900s and have long been criticized for their cruelty and inability to provide useful information.

The Draize Tests

The Draize tests attempt to measure the harmfulness of chemicals to humans by observing the damage they cause to the eyes and skin of animals. There are two kinds of Draize tests: the Draize eye irritancy test and the Draize skin irritancy test. Both cause extreme discomfort and pain to the animals involved. After the tests are completed, all of the animals are killed so that their internal organs can be examined.

In the Draize test for eye irritancy, solutions of products are applied directly into the animals' eyes, which can cause intense burning, itching and pain. Clips are placed on the eyelids to hold them open during the test period, which can last several days, and to keep the animals from blinking away the solution.

The animals are placed in restraining stocks that hold their heads in place, which prevents them from moving throughout the test period. In addition to causing terrible pain, the test compounds often leave the animals' eyes ulcerated and bleeding.

In the Draize test for skin irritancy, the test substances are applied to shaved and abraded skin, which is then covered with plastic sheeting. (Skin is abraded by firmly pressing adhesive tape onto the animal's body and quickly stripping it off. The process is repeated until several layers of skin have been removed.) As in the Draize eye irritancy test, these test solutions may cause intense pain, burning and itching.

The LD-50 Test

The LD-50 test is used to measure the acute toxicity levels of certain ingredients on live animals. LD-50 stands for Lethal Dose 50 Percent—the amount or concentration of a substance that will kill half of a test group of animals within a specified time period when that substance is forcibly ingested, inhaled or otherwise exposed to an animal.

During the LD-50 test period, the animals typically suffer extreme distress—pain, convulsions, vomiting, diarrhea and bleeding from the eyes and mouth. At the end of the test period, those animals that have not already died a painful and agonizing death are killed, and their internal organs are examined.

The classic LD-50 test has been banned in parts of Europe, and the U.S. Environmental Protection Agency (EPA) has announced that it no longer supports the use of this test.

Product testing on animals in no way protects public health and safety.

WHY TESTING PRODUCTS ON ANIMALS DOESN'T WORK

A deeply flawed research method produces false and misleading results.

The people who defend using animals to test products always say that these tests are necessary to protect the public. But there are plenty of products sitting on store shelves today that have been shown to be highly toxic, such as oven cleaners and permanent wave solutions. They simply have to carry a warning label and a childproof cap.

So, animal testing—much of which is done over and over again on products that have already been tested—does not eliminate potentially unsafe products from being introduced into the marketplace. And no amount of animal testing can change the fact that many of these products are harmful if ingested or used in a way not intended by the manufacturer. That is

why we say that animal testing is redundant and wasteful.

Moreover, there really isn't a reliable way of determining the amount of a product it would take to harm a human, or the specific ways in which it would do so, such as through an allergic reaction, based on the results of animal studies.

Animal testing is based on the belief that animals can "stand in" for human beings in the laboratory, and that the results of animal tests can be extrapolated to humans—that is, what *does* or *does not* work in a rat or rabbit will also *work* or *not work* in a human. But that's not necessarily so. Humans and animals are different in many ways—physiologically, anatomically, metabolically and psychologically.

.. animal tests fail to be *predictable*.

Animal testing:
a question of ethics

Those who defend animal testing contend that nonhuman animals are enough like us to make them scientifically adequate models, but different enough to make it ethically acceptable to use them as experimental subjects.

We disagree on both counts. Nonhuman animals are not similar enough to humans to make them adequate test models. But even if they were, we still oppose animal testing because it is morally unacceptable to exploit one species for the benefit of another.

With society progressing to the point where people from all walks of life are raising serious questions about the use and abuse of animals, we believe that a growing number of concerned citizens will begin to see that the pursuit of compassion is at least as important as the pursuit of knowledge.

Even the smallest difference in animals can have very different results in humans. As a result, sometimes animal tests work, and sometimes they don't. And no one can say for sure, until a human uses a product, what will happen. That is why animal tests fail to be *predictable*. Without predictability, animal tests are virtually useless.

THE SMART—AND HUMANE— SOLUTION TO ANIMAL TESTING

Non-animal testing methods produce more accurate and useful results.

It's an age-old question: What do we use if we stop using animals as test subjects? And there is a simple answer. Thanks to advancements in modern technology, there are now safe and reliable methods of testing products that save animal lives while assuring the safety and well-being of the public.

Proponents of non-animal testing methods in the scientific community have shown that these methods are often more reliable, quicker and cost-effective. Examples of these non-animal methods range from computer

Many companies avoid animal testing by referring to the U.S. "Generally Regarded As Safe" (GRAS), a list of thousands of ingredients already known to be safe. They also rely on data regarding historic use and chemical structure of a product or ingredient.

and mathematical models to the use of human volunteers. *In vitro* tests include ones that use cell or tissue cultures, such as artificial test skin derived from human foreskin. Chemical tests include the Neutral Red Bioassay that uses a neutral red, water-soluble dye that is added to normal skin cells in a tissue culture plate, and a computer measurement of the level of uptake of the dye by the cells is used to indicate the relative toxicity.

In addition to efforts by industry to develop and implement non-animal methods, other academic and private funding sources have been established to advance efforts to eliminate animal testing. The U.S. Interagency Coordinating Committee on the Validation of Alternative Methods (ICCVAM) was launched in 2000 with the passage of legislation passed unanimously by both houses of Congress. NAVS founded the International Foundation for Ethical Research (IFER) in 1985 to develop, validate and implement scientifically valid alternatives by providing grants to advance these objectives.

The validation and regulatory acceptance of non-animal alternative tests is critical to the adoption of more humane scientific methodologies. However, that process can be a long and arduous one. After a test is developed, it must go through a rigorous validation process before results from the test are regarded as reliable for general use. This validation process involves review and hearings by members of ICCVAM.

Unfortunately, despite broad support for the investment in the development and validation of alternatives, only a handful of methods have been officially validated.

There are many websites and bibliographic databases that detail the alternatives available, depending on the research topic. For more information, visit the NAVS website (www.navs.org), click on "Animals in Science," then click on "Science of the Future."

Learn about more non-animal alternatives used in product testing. Visit our website at **www.navs.org**, and click on "Animals in Product Testing," then click on "Alternatives."

WHY COMPANIES STILL TEST ON ANIMALS

Who's protecting whom when it comes to consumer safety.

By now you may be wondering why companies continue to test cosmetics, personal care, household, and companion animal products on live animals, when there are scientifically valid non-animal alternatives available and no regulations specifically mandating animal testing for these product categories.

That's a good question! To fully understand the answer, a bit of history is in order. In 1937, the S.E. Massengill Company decided to create a liquid form of the drug Sulfanilamide, which was being used to treat streptococcal infections (strep throat). The company's chief chemist developed a formulation that used diethlyene glycol as a medium for the liquid Sulfanilamide.

At the time, no one had any way of knowing that diethylene glycol is a deadly poison. Since no testing of pharmaceutical drugs was required at the time, the liquid Sulfanilamide was released to the public, and 107 people—mostly children—died.

The uproar that arose from this tragedy spurred Congress to pass the federal Food, Drug and Cosmetic Act. The U.S. Food and Drug Administration (FDA), which administers the Food, Drug and Cosmetic Act, requires that the results of animal tests be used as proof of the scientific safety of new pharmaceutical drugs and a number of chemical compounds that change the chemistry of the body before they can be marketed. However, the FDA does not require manufacturers of cosmetics to test on animals.

Nevertheless, the FDA urges companies to conduct whatever toxicological tests are appropriate to substantiate the safety of their products. Traditionally, manufacturers have used animal tests to provide this substantiation. And because animal testing is considered a standard, acceptable procedure, it has also become a convenient way for companies to make sure they have the appropriate safety data to present in court in the event of a lawsuit.

Even though companies have the option of using non-animal methodologies to produce safety data, many still feel that animal testing is their best legal safety net in these litigious times. Moreover, in a business climate that is becoming increasingly cost-conscious and competitive, companies often are reluctant to make the investment of time and money to explore alternatives.

Even though companies have the option of using non-animal methodologies to produce safety data, many still feel that animal testing is their best legal safety net in these litigious times.

DECODING THE LANGUAGE OF ANIMAL TESTING POLICIES

What is and isn't "cruelty free" can be a matter of interpretation.

At first glance, it would seem easy to determine whether a product is or isn't cruelty free. Has it, or has it not, been tested on animals? A simple yes or no would do.

Unfortunately, it's not that simple. The term "cruelty free" can mean different things to different people. Some cosmetic companies use the term "cruelty free" or "not tested on animals" to promote their products, but there is no legal definition for these terms. That means companies have unrestricted use of these phrases, which means they can use them to mean anything they want. That's why it's so important to be very wary of relying on product labels.

There's another complicating factor to determining what is and isn't "cruelty free." As animal advocates have become a stronger voice over the years, companies have become more elusive in answering questions about their animal testing policies. Naturally, companies want consumers to be comfortable buying their products, and they often lapse into "corporate-speak" when addressing the issue of animal testing with the public.

So how does the NAVS staff make proper designations when direct, straightforward answers are not always forthcoming? Sometimes, we have to read between the lines to determine where a company stands on the subject of animal testing. Others state their animal testing policies in a simple and direct manner. Some examples:

A statement from Elizabeth Arden:
"…we do not sponsor or perform any animal studies on our production formulations. This has been our policy since 1988. To avoid the use of tests on animals, our product development work involves materials with well-established safety records and the use of extensive ingredient databases. Our product safety testing also includes the use of non-animal studies, computer modeling and studies with human volunteers."

A statement from Revlon:
"Since June 1989, Revlon Consumer Products Corporation has not participated in animal testing. Revlon relies on the judgment of pharmacological, toxicological, and medical experts, non-animal alternative testing methods, and the past safety history of formulations and ingredients to determine product safety."

A statement from Estee Lauder:
"The Estee Lauder Companies utilizes state-of-the-art testing methods to insure the safety and efficacy of our products. All of our ingredients and formulations are tested in vitro and on human volunteers. We do not test our products on animals, nor do we ask others to conduct animal testing on our behalf. The Estee Lauder Companies has no intention of testing on animals in the future."

The direct statements regarding their products and formulations have earned these companies our "♥" designation of "cruelty free."

However, other corporate statements leave questions in our minds. Take, for example, a statement by L'Oreal, which says in part, *"We are happy to confirm that the L'Oreal group of companies, which includes Lancôme, Redken, Garnier, Ralph Lauren, Biotherm, and Helena Rubinstein, as well as L'Oreal, has carried out no animal testing since 1989 on the entire range of its products."*

Here is the policy statement from RoC® (which includes Johnson & Johnson Consumer Products Company, Neutrogena, and Personal Products Company): *"Final formulations for RoC® products are not tested on animals. However, individual ingredients may have in the past been tested on animals. Nowadays, new ingredients for RoC® products are skin-tested on human volunteers and final formulations continue not to be tested on animals."*

Both of these statements sound like the companies are cruelty free. But they make no mention of whether or not their suppliers conduct animal tests. What's more, while they say that the company itself doesn't test on animals, the wording is such that there's no way to tell whether or not they have outsourced animal testing to an independent laboratory, which companies often do. As a result, we have placed these companies in the "◆" category of "does not test on animals, but has no formal agreement with suppliers that they do not test on animals."

Then there are cases where a company, in addition to manufacturing cosmetics, also makes other products, which must be tested on animals. For example, the Dial Corporation's corporate policy states:
"The Dial Corporation does not use animals in evaluating the safety of our non-food products (except when required by law). We rely on published data and non-animal alternative testing to confirm the safety of ingredients."

The Gillette Company is another example. They state: *"During the reporting periods since October 1, 1995, no laboratory animals were used to validate the safety of Gillette non-pharmaceutical products."*

In the case of both The Dial Corporation and The Gillette Company, we have designated them as testers, because a part of the corporation does indeed test on animals, even though their non-food/non-pharmaceutical products are not animal-tested. Our philosophy is that if a company harms a single animal, they receive the "▼" designation—"tester."

However, in these cases, it's up to you as to where you want to draw the line. You may be willing to compromise with a company like Dial or Gillette. It's your own personal decision.

Then there is the last category— **DNR**, which stands for Did Not Respond. These are companies that have not responded to our survey, as well as our follow-up calls and e-mails. It's important to remember that even though a company did not respond to our inquiries, it does not necessarily mean that they are a tester. Today, more and more companies are very cautious of being associated in any way with animal advocacy groups, and therefore do not wish to be listed in our directory.

We hope that this section has provided you some insight into the many issues involving how a product is termed "cruelty free" and how we make the determinations that we do. Hopefully, the day when we can designate *all* companies as cruelty free is not too far in the distant future.

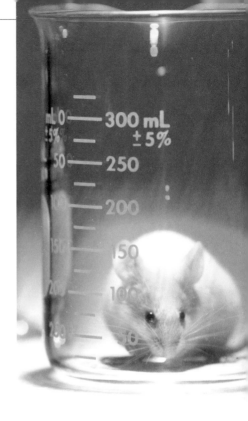

It's important to remember that even though a company did not respond to our inquiries, it does not necessarily mean that they are a tester.

Use Your

Directory of Cruelty-Free Products by Product Type   26

How to Use the Main Directory   36

Directory of Companies That DO and DO NOT Test on Animals   38

DIRECTORY OF CRUELTY-FREE PRODUCTS BY PRODUCT TYPE

If you're shopping for a particular type of product, such as bathroom cleaners or shaving products, this section lists cruelty-free companies by product type in a variety of categories as a quick and easy reference.

Due to space constraints, individual products are not listed here. To look up an individual product or brand name, check the main directory that begins on page 38.

Air Fresheners

Aubrey Organics
Earth Friendly Products
Orange-Mate Inc.
WiseWays Herbals

All Purpose Cleaners

Allens Naturally
Amazon Premium Products
Aubrey Organics

Bio Pac Inc.
Bi-O-Kleen Industries, Inc.
Dr. Bronner's Magic Soaps
Earth Essentials
Earth Friendly Products
Earthly Matters
Frank T. Ross & Sons, Ltd.
Orange-Mate Inc.
Planet Inc.
Seventh Generation
Shaklee Corp.
Vermont Soapworks

Aromatherapy

Alexandra Avery Purely Natural
Arbonne Int'l
Auroma Int'l, Inc.
Auromere Ayurvedic Imports
Avalon Natural Products
Body Time
Earth Essentials
Elizabeth Van Buren Inc.
Essential 3 (formerly
    Jacki's Magic Lotion)

Mountain Rose Herbs
Smith & Vandiver, Inc.
Stick-With-Us Products, Inc.

Baby Products

Arbonne Int'l
Aubrey Organics
Great Mother's Goods
Jurlique Holistic Skin Corp. USA
MediPatch Laboratories Corp.
Mountain Rose Herbs
Natracare LLC
Seventh Generation
Shaklee Corp.
TerrEssentials
VeganEssentials

Bath Products

Alexandra Avery Purely Natural
Aubrey Organics
Auromere Ayurvedic Imports
Avalon Natural Products
Avon Products, Inc.
Body Time
Clearly Natural Products
Dermalogica, Inc.
Dr. Hauschka Skin Care, Inc.

Earth Essentials
Garden Botanika
Gerda Spillmann USA
Great Mother's Goods
Honeybee Gardens
Lucky Chick
MediPatch Laboratories Corp.
Mountain Rose Herbs
Nutribiotic
Prima Fleur Botanicals, Inc.
Pure Touch Therapeutics
Simmons Natural Bodycare
Smith & Vandiver, Inc.
St. Ives Laboratories
St. John's Herb Garden, Inc.
TARRAH Cosmetics
TerrEssentials
The Body Shop
Universal Light
VeganEssentials
Vermont Soapworks
V'tae Parfume & Body Care
WiseWays Herbals

Bathroom Cleaners

Amazon Premium Products
Bio Pac Inc.
Earth Friendly Products
Seventh Generation

Carpet/Rug Care

Fleabusters/Rx for Fleas, Inc.

Companion Animal Care

Allerpet, Inc.
Aubrey Organics
Blue Ribbons Pet Care
Burns Pet Nutrition
Dr. Goodpet
Espree Animal Products, Inc.
Fleabusters/Rx for Fleas, Inc.
MediPatch Laboratories Corp.
New Methods
Sunfeather Natural Soap Co.
VeganEssentials
Vermont Soapworks
V'tae Parfume & Body Care
WiseWays Herbals

Companion Animal Food

Wow-Bow Distributors, Ltd.

Contact Lens Care

Clear Conscience, LLC

Cosmetics

Almay, Inc.
Arbonne Int'l
Aubrey Organics
Avalon Natural Products
Avon Products, Inc.
Carma Laboratories, Inc.
Chanel, Inc.
CiCi Cosmetics
Color My Image Inc.
Dermalogica, Inc.
Elizabeth Arden, Inc.
Estee Lauder Companies
Gabriel Cosmetics, Inc.
Garden Botanika
Gerda Spillmann USA
Hard Candy
Jurlique Holistic Skin Corp. USA
Liz Claiborne Inc.
Louise Bianco Skin Care, Inc.
Lucky Chick
Marilyn Miglin, L.P.
Mary Kay Corp.
Orlane, Inc.
Paul Penders Co., Inc.

Pout
Revlon, Inc.
Shaklee Corp.
TARRAH Cosmetics
The Body Shop
Urban Decay
VeganEssentials
Zhen, Inc.
Zia Natural Skincare

Deodorants/Antiperspirants

Aubrey Organics
Avalon Natural Products
Avon Products, Inc.
Nutribiotic
Shaklee Corp.
TCCD Int'l, Inc.
TerrEssentials
Tom's of Maine, Inc.

Depilatories

Stick-With-Us Products, Inc.

Diapers

Seventh Generation

Dishwashing Products

Allens Naturally
Bio Pac Inc.
Bi-O-Kleen Industries, Inc.
Earth Essentials
Earth Friendly Products
Planet Inc.
Seventh Generation
Shaklee Corp.

Feminine Hygiene

Alberto Culver
Mountain Rose Herbs
Natracare LLC
Simmons Natural Bodycare

First Aid

Lifeline Co.
Nutribiotic
WiseWays Herbals

Foot Care

Avon Products, Inc.
Freeman Beauty
Garden Botanika
Gerda Spillmann USA

Lucky Chick
Nutribiotic
Smith & Vandiver, Inc.
Stick-With-Us Products, Inc.
TARRAH Cosmetics
TCCD Int'l, Inc.
Wisdom Oral Care, Ltd.
   (formerly CP2 Distribution, LLC)

Fragrances

Alexandra Avery Purely Natural
Arbonne Int'l
Aubrey Organics
Avon Products, Inc.
Body Time
Chanel, Inc.
Chishti Co.
Eden Botanicals
Elizabeth Arden, Inc.
Estee Lauder Companies
Garden Botanika
Hard Candy
Liz Claiborne Inc.
Marilyn Miglin, L.P.
Mary Kay Corp.
Master's Flower Essences
Orlane, Inc.
Parlux Fragrances, Inc.

Revlon, Inc.
Simmons Natural Bodycare
Smith & Vandiver, Inc.
St. John's Herb Garden, Inc.
The Body Shop
VeganEssentials
V'tae Parfume & Body Care

Furniture Cleaners

Amazon Premium Products
Earth Friendly Products
WiseWays Herbals

Hair Care

Alberto Culver
Arbonne Int'l
Aubrey Organics
Avalon Natural Products
Avon Products, Inc.
Bio Pac Inc.
Body Time
Dermalogica, Inc.
Estee Lauder Companies
Frank T. Ross & Sons, Ltd.
Freeman Beauty
Garden Botanika
Honeybee Gardens

Jason Natural Products
Magick Botanicals
Mountain Ocean Ltd.
Mountain Rose Herbs
Nexxus Products Co.
Paul Penders Co., Inc.
Prima Fleur Botanicals, Inc.
Pure Touch Therapeutics
Revlon, Inc.
Shaklee Corp.
ShiKai Products
Simmons Natural Bodycare
St. Ives Laboratories
TARRAH Cosmetics
TerrEssentials
The Body Shop
Tom's of Maine, Inc.
Universal Light
VeganEssentials

Hair Coloring

Estee Lauder Companies
Revlon, Inc.

Insect Repellents

Avon Products, Inc.
V'tae Parfume & Body Care

Laundry Products

Allens Naturally
Amazon Premium Products
Bio Pac Inc.
Bi-O-Kleen Industries, Inc.
Earth Essentials
Earth Friendly Products
Frank T. Ross & Sons, Ltd.
Planet Inc.
Seventh Generation
Shaklee Corp.

Massage Products

Arbonne Int'l
Auroma Int'l, Inc.
Avalon Natural Products
Earth Essentials
Eden Botanicals
Essential 3 (formerly
  Jacki's Magic Lotion)
Gerda Spillmann USA
Lakon Herbals
Mountain Ocean Ltd.
Mountain Rose Herbs
Prima Fleur Botanicals, Inc.
Pure Touch Therapeutics
St. John's Herb Garden, Inc.

V'tae Parfume & Body Care
Windrose Trading Co.
WiseWays Herbals

Nail Care

Avon Products, Inc.
Dermalogica, Inc.
Gerda Spillmann USA
Hard Candy
Honeybee Gardens
Mary Kay Corp.
Urban Decay

Oral Care

Aubrey Organics
Auromere Ayurvedic Imports
Eco-Dent Int'l, Inc.
Jason Natural Products
Mountain Rose Herbs
Shaklee Corp.
Tom's of Maine, Inc.
Wisdom Oral Care, Ltd.
   (formerly CP2 Distribution, LLC)
Woodstock Natural Products, Inc.

Paper Products

Earth Friendly Products
Seventh Generation

Shaving Products

Avalon Natural Products
Dermalogica, Inc.
Honeybee Gardens
Simmons Natural Bodycare
Tom's of Maine, Inc.

Skin Care

Alberto Culver
Alexandra Avery Purely Natural
Arbonne Int'l
Aubrey Organics
Auroma Int'l, Inc.
Auromere Ayurvedic Imports
Avalon Natural Products
Avon Products, Inc.
Aztec Secret
Bio Pac Inc.
Biogime Skincare, Inc.
Body Time
Borlind of Germany
Chanel, Inc.
Clearly Natural Products

Color My Image Inc.
Derma E
Dermalogica, Inc.
Dr. Bronner's Magic Soaps
Dr. Hauschka Skin Care, Inc.
Earth Essentials
Elizabeth Arden, Inc.
Elizabeth Van Buren Inc.
Essential 3 (formerly
  Jacki's Magic Lotion)
Estee Lauder Companies
Frank T. Ross & Sons, Ltd.
Freeman Beauty
Gabriel Cosmetics, Inc.
Garden Botanika
Gerda Spillmann USA
Great Mother's Goods
Honeybee Gardens
Jason Natural Products
Jelene, Inc.
Jurlique Holistic Skin Corp. USA
Kirk's Natural Products Corp.
Lakon Herbals
Louise Bianco Skin Care, Inc.
Lucky Chick
Mad Gab's
Magick Botanicals
Marilyn Miglin, L.P.

Mary Kay Corp.
Mountain Ocean Ltd.
Mountain Rose Herbs
Nexxus Products Co.
Niora
Norimoor Co., Inc.
Nutribiotic
Orlane, Inc.
Paul Penders Co., Inc.
Prima Fleur Botanicals, Inc.
Pure Touch Therapeutics
Revlon, Inc.
Shaklee Corp.
ShiKai Products
Simmons Natural Bodycare
Smith & Vandiver, Inc.
St. Ives Laboratories
Stick-With-Us Products, Inc.
Sunfeather Natural Soap Co.
TARRAH Cosmetics
TCCD Int'l, Inc.
TerrEssentials
The Body Shop
Tom's of Maine, Inc.
Universal Light
Urban Decay
VeganEssentials
Vermont Soapworks

V'tae Parfume & Body Care
WiseWays Herbals
Zhen, Inc.
Zia Natural Skincare

Stain Removers

Amazon Premium Products
Bio Pac Inc.
Bi-O-Kleen Industries, Inc.
Earth Friendly Products

Sun Care

Arbonne Int'l
Aubrey Organics
Avalon Natural Products
Avon Products, Inc.
Borlind of Germany
Dermalogica, Inc.
Estee Lauder Companies
Gerda Spillmann USA
Jason Natural Products
Mary Kay Corp.
Mountain Ocean Ltd.
The Body Shop
V'tae Parfume & Body Care
Zia Natural Skincare

Companies to contact:

How to Use the Main Directory

The main section of this book, which contains the listing of companies and brand names that do and do not test their products and/or the ingredients in their products on animals, begins on page 38.

Each listing includes one of the following symbols in front of the company name:

❤ Company is cruelty free. It does not test its final products or ingredients on animals, and it has a formal agreement with its outside suppliers that they also do not test on animals. A company can only be listed as cruelty free if it meets all these requirements.

🌿 Subsidiary/division does not test its final products or ingredients on animals, even though its parent company may test on animals. To receive this designation, the subsidiary/division must also have a formal agreement from its suppliers confirming that they also do not test on animals.

◆ The company does not test its final products or ingredients on animals, but it has no formal agreement with its suppliers stating that they do not test their products or ingredients on animals.

▼ Company does test its final products and/or ingredients on animals.

DNR Company did not respond to the original NAVS survey or any follow-up correspondence. However, this does not necessarily mean that the company tests their products and/or ingredients on animals.

If a company is not listed, it means we are unaware of it and therefore have not had the opportunity to send them our survey.

For an explanation of how we interpret the often vague language of some companies' animal testing policies to make our designations, see page 20.

Each listing may also include one or more of the following symbols after the company name:

❋ Company manufactures and/or sells products that are *vegan*—that is, they do not contain animal by-products, such as beeswax, lanolin or gelatin. For a complete listing of animal-derived ingredients, see page 154.

■ Company is a manufacturer.

▣ Company is a mail order company. They may or may not manufacture products and may also feature products from many sources. Products can be purchased via catalogs, phone or Internet. For a listing of cruelty-free mail order companies, turn to page 148.

❤ ☙ ◆ ▼ DNR
❋ ■ ▣

All these symbols are repeated on the fold-out back flap of this book, which makes a great placeholder when you're shopping!

37

DIRECTORY OF COMPANIES THAT DO AND DO NOT TEST ON ANIMALS

▼ 20 Mule Team
(see Dial Corp., Inc.)

DNR 3M™
3M Center
St. Paul, MN 55144-1000
(888) 364-3577; (651) 733-1110
www.3m.com

▼ A Touch of Sun
(see Procter & Gamble)

◆ A.C.T. (Anti-Chlorine-Treatment)
(see Dena Corp.)

DNR A.J. Funk & Co.
1471 Timber Dr.
Elgin, IL 60123
(847) 741-6760
www.glasscleaner.com

DNR ABBA Pure & Natural Hair Care
7400 E. Tierra Buena Ln.
Scottsdale, AZ 85260
(800) 933-4303
www.framesi.it
(see Framesi USA)

DNR ABCO, Inc.
2450 S. Watney Way #2519
Fairfield, CA 94533-6730
(800) 678-2226

DNR Abra Therapeutics
10365 Hwy. 116
Forestville, CA 95436
(707) 869-0761
www.abratherapeutics.com

♥ Absolutely Fabulous fragrance
(see Revlon, Inc.)

▼ Acuvue
(see Johnson & Johnson)

DNR Adra Natural Soap
7955 Silverton Ave., Ste. 1201
San Diego, CA 92126-6343
(800) 984-7627
www.adrasoap.com

DNR Adrien Arpel
(see Color Me Beautiful, Inc.)

DNR Advanced Research Laboratories
151 Kalmus Dr., Ste. H-3
Costa Mesa, CA 92626
(800) 966-6960; (714) 556-1028
www.advreslab.com

DNR African Royale
(see Bronner Brothers)

▼ Afta
(see Colgate-Palmolive Co.)

▼ Agility
(see Gillette Co.)

▼ Agree
(see Schwarzkopf & Dep Inc.)

DNR AHAVA
124 McQueen Blvd. Industrial Park
Summerville, SC 29483
(800) 25-AHAVA; (843) 875-7347
www.ahava.com

▼ Aim
(see Church & Dwight Co., Inc.)

◆ Air Scense
(see Citra-Solv, LLC)

DNR Air Therapy
(see Mia Rose Products, Inc.)

▼ Air Wick
(see Reckitt-Benckiser plc)

DNR Airoma Mister
(see Mia Rose Products, Inc.)

▼ Aiyana hair care
(see Oxyfresh Worldwide, Inc.)

▼ Ajax products
(see Colgate-Palmolive Co.)

DNR AKA Saunders, Inc./TerraNova
1011 Gilman St.
Berkeley, CA 94710
(800) 966-3457; (510) 558-7100
www.terranovabody.com

❤ Alba Botanica
(see Avalon Natural Products)

❤ Alberto Culver ■
2525 Armitage Ave.
Melrose Park, IL 60160-1163
(708) 450-3000
www.alberto.com
Household, Personal Care

DNR Alcone, Inc.
5-49 49th Ave.
Long Island City, NY 11101
(800) 466-7446; (718) 361-8373
www.alconeco.com

♥ Alexandra Avery Purely Natural ■ ⋯
4717 SE Belmont
Portland, OR 97215
(800) 669-1863; (503) 236-5926
www.alexandraavery.com
Cosmetics, Personal Care

▼ All detergent
(see Unilever)

DNR All Terrain Co.
315 1st St., Ste. U-274
Encinitas, CA 92024-3528
(800) 246-7328
www.allterrainco.com

▼ Alldays
(see Procter & Gamble)

♥ Allens Naturally ✳ ■ ⋯
P.O. Box 514
Farmington, MI 48332-0339
(248) 449-7708
www.allensnaturally.com
Household

♥ Allerpet, Inc. ✳ ■
P.O. Box 2220, Lenox Hill Stn.
New York, NY 10021
(212) 861-1134
www.allerpet.com
Companion Animal Care

♥ Almay, Inc. ■
625 Madison Ave.
New York, NY 10022
(800) 992-5629
www.almay.com
Cosmetics
(see Revlon, Inc.)

DNR Aloe Commodities Inc.
2161 Hutton Dr., Ste. 126
Carrollton, TX 75006-0333
(972) 241-4251

♦ Aloe Complete ✳ ■
P.O. Box 67
Vista, CA 92085-0067
(800) 464-2563
Cosmetics, Personal Care

DNR Aloe Creme Laboratories
160 Meister Ave.
North Branch, NJ 08876
(800) 327-4969
www.aloecreme.com

DNR Aloette Cosmetics, Inc.
4900 Highlands Pkwy. SE
Smyrna, GA 30082-5132
(800) ALOETTE; (770) 956-9700
www.aloettecosmetics.com

▼ Always
(see Procter & Gamble)

❤ Amazon Premium Products ❋ ■ ▫
275 NE 59th St.
Miami, FL 33137
(800) 832-5645
www.amazonpp.com
Household

DNR Ambi Pur
(see Sara Lee Corp.)

DNR American Brand Labs
5310 Beethoven St.
Los Angeles, CA 90066-7015
(800) 669-9514; (310) 574-6920
www.aromavera.com

DNR American Crew
1732 Champa St.
Denver, CO 80202
(800) 598-CREW
www.americancrew.com

DNR American Formulating & Mfg.
3251 3rd Ave.
San Diego, CA 92103-5615
(619) 239-0321
www.afmsafecoat.com

◆ American Int'l Ind. ■
2220 Gaspar Ave.
Los Angeles, CA 90040
(800) 621-9585; (323) 728-4464
www.aiibeauty.com
Cosmetics, Personal Care

DNR American Safety Razor Co.
240 Cedar Knolls Rd.
Cedar Knolls, NJ 07927
(800) 445-9284; (973) 753-3000
www.asrco.com

DNR America's Finest Products Corp.
1639 9th St.
Santa Monica, CA 90404
(310) 450-6555

DNR Amrita Aromatherapy, Inc.
1900 W. Stone Ave.
Fairfield, IA 52556-2152
(641) 472-9136
www.amrita.net

▼ Amway Corp. ■
7575 Fulton St. East
Ada, MI 49355-0001
(616) 787-6000
www.amway.com
Household, Personal Care

◆ Andrea Int'l ■
2220 Gaspar Ave.
Los Angeles, CA 90040
(323) 728-2999
www.aiibeauty.com
Cosmetics, Personal Care
(see American Int'l Ind.)

▼ Angel Soft
(see Georgia-Pacific)

❤ Annemarie Borlind
(see Borlind of Germany)

▼ Answer Pregnancy and
Ovulation Tests
(see Church & Dwight Co., Inc.)

DNR Aqua Velva
(see Sara Lee Corp.)

▼ Aquafresh
(see GlaxoSmithKline
Consumer Healthcare)

❤ Aramis
(see Estee Lauder Companies)

◆ Arbico Environmental ✳ ■ ⊡
P.O. Box 8910
Tucson, AZ 85738-0910
(800) 827-2847 (520) 825-9785
www.arbico.com
Companion Animal Care, Household

❤ Arbonne Int'l ✳ ■ ⊡
9400 Jeronimo
Irvine, CA 92618
(800) ARBONNE; (949) 770-2610
www.arbonne.com
Cosmetics, Personal Care

◆ Ardell Int'l ■
2220 Gaspar Ave.
Los Angeles, CA 90040
(323) 728-2999
www.aiibeauty.com
Cosmetics, Personal Care
(see American Int'l Ind.)

❤ Ardenbeauty
(see Elizabeth Arden, Inc.)

◆ Arizona Natural Resources ✳■
2525 E. Beardsley Rd.
Phoenix, AZ 85050
(602) 569-6900
www.aznaturals.com
Cosmetics, Household, Personal Care

▼ Arm & Hammer
(see Church & Dwight Co., Inc.)

▼ Armstrong floor cleaner
(see S.C. Johnson)

DNR Aroma Clear
(see Sunshine Makers, Inc.)

DNR Aroma Medica
900 Bethlehem Pike
Glenside, PA 19038-7702
(215) 233-5210
www.aromamedica.com

DNR Aroma Terra
2432 W. Peoria Ave., Bldg. 10,
Ste. 1183
Phoenix, AZ 85029
(602) 371-4676
www.aromaterra.com

DNR Aromaland, Inc.
1326 Rufina Cir.
Santa Fe, NM 87505
(800) 933-5267; (505) 438-0402
www.buyaromatherapy.com

◆ AromaTherapeutix ■▣
P.O. Box 2908
Seal Branch, CA 90740
(800) 308-6284
Personal Care

DNR Arran Aromatics
(see Esscentual Brands, LLC)

▼ Arrid
(see Church & Dwight Co., Inc.)

◆ ARTec
(see L'Oreal)

DNR Artmatic cosmetics
(see Markwins International Corp.
(formerly AM Cosmetics))

DNR At Last Naturals
401 Columbus Ave.
Valhalla, NY 10595
(800) 527-8123
www.atlastnaturals.com

▼ Atra
(see Gillette Co.)

❤ Atrevida fragrance
(see Marilyn Miglin, L.P.)

DNR Atzen
1790 Hamilton Ave.
San Jose, CA 95125
(800) 468-4362; (408) 265-0121
www.atzen.com

❤ Aubrey Organics ✳ ■ ▣
4419 N. Manhattan Ave.
Tampa, FL 33614
(800) 282-7394; (813) 877-4186
www.aubrey-organics.com
*Companion Animal Care, Cosmetics,
Household, Personal Care*

❤ Auroma Int'l, Inc. ✳ ■
P.O. Box 1008
Silver Lake, WI 53170
(262) 889-8569
www.auromaintl.com
Household, Personal Care

❤ Auromere Ayurvedic Imports ✳ ▣
2621 W. Hwy. 12
Lodi, CA 95242
(800) 735-4691; (209) 339-3710
www.auromere.com
Personal Care

◆ Aurora Henna Co. ■ ▣
5010 Hwy 169 N
New Hope, MN 55428
(763) 592-4770
*Companion Animal Care,
Personal Care*

▼ Aussie products
(see Procter & Gamble)

❤ Avalon Natural Products ■ ▣
1105 Industrial Ave.
Petaluma, CA 94952
(707) 347-1200
www.avalonorganics.com
Cosmetics, Personal Care

❤ Avalon Organic Botanicals
(see Avalon Natural Products)

❤ Avalon Organics
(see Avalon Natural Products)

♥ Aveda
(see Estee Lauder Companies)

▼ Aveeno
(see Johnson & Johnson)

◆ Avicenna Labs, Inc. ✻ ■
850 Nicholas Blvd.
Elk Grove Village, IL 60007
(847) 640-2771
www.denacorp.com
Personal Care
(see Dena Corp.)

♥ Avon Products, Inc. ■
1345 Ave of the Americas
New York, NY 10105-0302
(800) 367-2866; (212) 282-5000
www.avon.com
Cosmetics, Personal Care

▼ Axe deodorant
(see Unilever)

DNR Axel Kraft
99 Engelhard Dr.
Aurora, Ontario, Canada L4G 3V
(800) 667-7864; (905) 841-6840
www.axelkraft.com

DNR Azida, Inc.
4078 S. Hohokam Dr.
Sierra Vista, AZ 85650-8590
(800) 603-6601
www.azida.com

♥ Aztec Secret ✻ ■
P.O. Box 841
Pahrump, NV 89041-0841
(775) 727-1882
www.aztec-secret.com
Personal Care

DNR Azur Fragrances USA, Inc.
50 E. 42nd St., Ste. 2105
New York, NY 10017
(212) 687-5566
www.azur-fragrances.com

DNR Baby Magic
(see Playtex Products, Inc.)

❧ Back to Basics
(see Graham Webb)

DNR Back to Nature, Inc.
5627 N. Milwaukee Ave.
Chicago, IL 60646
(773) 463-5758
www.back2nature.net

▼ Bain de Soleil
(see Schering-Plough Corp.)

▼ Balmex
(see Johnson & Johnson)

▼ Balsam Color
(see Procter & Gamble)

◆ Ban
(see Kao Brands Co. (formerly
Andrew Jergens Co.))

DNR Banana Boat
(see Playtex Products, Inc.)

DNR Banana Republic fragrances
(see Gap, Inc.)

▼ Band-Aid
(see Johnson & Johnson)

DNR Bar Keepers Friend
(see SerVaas Laboratories Inc.)

DNR Bare Escentuals
425 Bush St., 3rd Fl.
San Francisco, CA 94108
(800) 227-3990; (415) 288-3500
www.bareescentuals.com

❤ Bare Foot
(see Freeman Beauty)

DNR Basch Co., Inc.
P.O. Box 188
Freeport, NY 11520
(516) 378-8100

DNR Bath & Body Works
7 Limited Pkwy. East
Reynoldsburg, OH 43068-5300
(800) 395-1001; (614) 856-6000
www.BathandBodyWorks.com
(see Limited, Inc.)

DNR Bath Island, Inc.
469 Amsterdam Ave.
New York, NY 10024
(212) 787-9415
www.bathisland.com

DNR Batherapy
(see Para Laboratories, Inc.)

DNR Baudelaire, Inc.
170 Emerald St.
Keene, NH 03431
(800) 327-2324; (603) 352-9234
www.baudelairesoaps.com

▼ Bausch & Lomb Inc. ■
1400 N. Goodman St.
Rochester, NY 14609
(800) 344-8815; (585) 338-6000
www.bausch.com
Personal Care

DNR BB products
(see Bronner Brothers)

▼ BCBG Max Azria fragrances
(see Unilever)

◆ Beach Blonde
(see Kao Brands Co. (formerly
Andrew Jergens Co.))

DNR Beaumont Products, Inc.
1560 Big Shanty Dr.
Kennesaw, GA 30144
(800) 451-7096; (770) 514-9000
www.citrusmagic.com

DNR Beauty For All Seasons, Inc.
P.O. Box 1950
La Puente, CA 91749-1950
(800) 942-4336

DNR Beauty Naturally, Inc.
P.O. Box 4905
Burlingame, CA 94010
(650) 697-1809
www.beautynaturally.com

DNR Beauty Without Cruelty
(see Natural Resource Group)

◆ Beiersdorf, Inc. ■
187 Danbury Rd.
Wilton, CT 06897
(800) 227-4703; (203) 563-5800
www.beiersdorf.com
Personal Care

◆ Belle Star, Inc. ✻ ■ ▨
1021 S. Linwood Ave.
Santa Ana, CA 92705
(714) 647-0012
www.belle-star.com
Cosmetics, Personal Care

◆ Ben Nye Co. ■
5935 Bowcroft St.
Los Angeles, CA 90016
(310) 839-1984
Cosmetics

DNR BeneFit cosmetics
(see LVMH Moet Hennessy Louis Vuitton)

DNR Bengay
(see Pfizer)

DNR Benjamin Ansehl Co.
15 Sunnen Dr., Ste. 115
Saint Louis, MO 63143-3819
(800) 937-2284

DNR BIC Corp.
500 BIC Dr.
Milford, CT 06460
(203) 783-2000
www.bicworld.com

DNR Bijan Fragrances, Inc.
510A N. Sheridan St.
Corona, CA 92880
(800) 99-BIJAN
www.bijan.com

DNR Bikini Bare
(see Lee Pharmaceuticals)

DNR Bikini Zone
(see CCA Industries, Inc.)

DNR Binaca
(see Playtex Products, Inc.)

❤ Binge
(see Freeman Beauty)

❤ Bio Pac Inc. ✳■
584 Pinto Ct.
Incline Village, NV 89451
(800) 225-2855
www.bio-pac.com
Household

DNR Biocide, Inc.
P.O. Box 3246
Stamford, CT 06905-0246
(203) 329-7705

DNR BioFilm, Inc.
3121 Scott St.
Vista, CA 92083-8323
(800) 848-5900; (760) 727-9030
www.astroglide.com

❤ Biogime Skincare, Inc. ✳■▣
25602 I-45 North, Ste. 106
Spring, TX 77386
(800) 338-8784; (281) 298-2607
www.biogimeskincare.com
Cosmetics, Personal Care

DNR Bionutrient
(see NIOXIN Research
Laboratories, Inc.)

❤ Bi-O-Kleen Industries, Inc. ❁ ■
P.O. Box 820689
Vancouver, WA 98682
(800) 477-0188; (360) 576-0064
www.bi-o-kleen.com
Household

◆ Bioré products
(see Kao Brands Co. (formerly
Andrew Jergens Co.))

◆ Biotherm
(see L'Oreal)

DNR Biotone Professional Massage
Products
4757 Old Cliffs Rd.
San Diego, CA 92120
(800) 445-6457
www.biotone.com

DNR Bissell, Inc.
2345 Walker, NW
Grand Rapids, WI 49544
(616) 453-4451
www.bissell.com

DNR Black Radiance cosmetics
(see Markwins International Corp.
(formerly AM Cosmetics))

DNR Blistex, Inc.
1800 Swift Dr.
Oak Brook, IL 60523
(630) 571-2870
www.blistex.com

DNR Bloom Cosmetics
1205 Hilltop Pkwy.
Steamboat Springs, CO 80487
www.bloomcosmetics.com

DNR Blue Coral-Slick 50, Ltd.
5700 S. Lee Rd.
Cleveland, OH 44137
(800) 321-8577; (216) 332-4200
www.bluecoral.com

DNR Blue Cross Beauty Products, Inc.
12251 Montague St.
Pacoima, CA 91331
(818) 896-8681

DNR Blue Cross Laboratories
26411 Golden Valley Rd.
Santa Clarita, CA 91350
(661) 255-0955
www.bc-labs.com

♥ Blue Ribbons Pet Care ✳ ■ ▣
9 Twin Pine Ln.
Center Moriches, NY 11934
(800) 552-BLUE; (631) 968-9164
www.blueribbonspetcare.com
Companion Animal Care

DNR Bob Kelly Cosmetics, Inc.
151 W. 46th St.
New York, NY 10036
(212) 819-0030

♥ Bobbi Brown
(see Estee Lauder Companies)

DNR Bocabelli Soap
4004 Avondale Ln.
Canton, OH 44708-1618
(330) 477-9048
www.bocabelli.com

♦ Body Drench ■
2220 Gaspar Ave.
Los Angeles, CA 90040
(323) 728-2999
www.aiibeauty.com
Cosmetics, Personal Care
(see American Int'l Ind.)

DNR Body Encounters
230 N. Maple Ave.
Marlton, NJ 08053
(800) 839-2639; (856) 985-6363
www.bodyencounters.com

♥ Body Time ▣
1101 Eighth St., Ste. 100
Berkeley, CA 94710
(510) 524-0216
www.bodytime.com
Personal Care

DNR Bodyography
1641 16th St.
Santa Monica, CA 90404
(310) 399-2886
www.bodyography.com

DNR BodyZone Skin Organics
P.O. Box 66457
Los Angeles, CA 90066
(800) 262-2616

▼ Bold
(see Procter & Gamble)

DNR Bonne Bell, Inc.
18519 Detroit Ave.
Lakewood, OH 44107
(800) 321-1006; (216) 221-0800
www.bonnebell.com

▼ Borateem
(see Dial Corp., Inc.)

❤ Borlind of Germany ■
P.O. Box 130
New London, NH 03257
(800) 447-7024; (603) 526-2076
www.borlind.com
Cosmetics

▼ Born Blonde
(see Procter & Gamble)

▼ Boston products
(see Bausch & Lomb Inc.)

DNR Botanicus Inc.
7610 Rickenbacker Dr., Ste. T
Gaithersburg, MD 20879
(800) 282-8887; (301) 977-8887
www.the-rubb.com

❤ Botopical
(see Freeman Beauty)

▼ Bounce
(see Procter & Gamble)

▼ Bounty
(see Procter & Gamble)

DNR Bradford Soap Works, Inc.
P.O. Box 1007
200 Providence St.
West Warwick, RI 02893
(401) 821-2141
www.bradfordsoap.com

▼ Brasso
(see Reckitt-Benckiser plc)

▼ Braun
(see Gillette Co.)

▼ Brawny
(see Georgia-Pacific)

DNR Breath-Eze
(see St. JON Laboratories)

◆ Brilliant Brunette
(see Kao Brands Co. (formerly Andrew Jergens Co.))

▼ Brillo
(see Church & Dwight Co., Inc.)

◆ Brillo household cleaners
(see USA Detergents)

DNR Bristol-Myers Squibb Co.
345 Park Ave.
New York, NY 10154-0037
(212) 546-4000
www.bms.com

▼ Brita
(see Clorox Co.)

▼ Brite
(see S.C. Johnson)

❤ Britney Spear's Curious
by Britney Spears
(see Elizabeth Arden, Inc.)

DNR Brocato
1 Main St., Ste. 501
Minneapolis, MN 55414
(800) 243-0275
www.brocatouk.com

DNR Bronner Brothers
600 Bronner Brothers Way
Atlanta, GA 30310
(404) 696-4000
www.bronnerbros.com

◆ Brookside Herbal Soap Co. ■
1340-G Industrial Ave.
Petaluma, CA 94952
(707) 763-0662
www.brooksidesoap.com
Personal Care

DNR Brucci, Ltd.
861 Nepperham Ave.
Yonkers, NY 10703
(914) 965-0707
www.brucci.com

▼ Brut
(see Unilever)

DNR Brylcreem
(see Sara Lee Corp.)

DNR Buf-Puf
(see 3M™)

DNR Bull Frog
(see Chattem, Inc.)

❤ Bumble and bumble
(see Estee Lauder Companies)

DNR Bump Fighter
(see American Safety Razor Co.)

DNR Burma-Shave
(see American Safety Razor Co.)

❤ Burns Pet Nutrition ■
4 Avalon Court
Kidwelly, S. Wales, SA17 5EJ
(219) 983-9651; 01554 890482
www.burns-pet-nutrition.co.uk
Companion Animal Care

DNR Burt's Bees
P.O. Box 13489
Durham, NC 27709
(800) 849-7112; (919) 998-5200
www.burtsbees.com

DNR Buty-Wave Products Co., Inc.
7323 Beverly Blvd.
Los Angeles, CA 90036
(323) 936-2191

DNR C.E. Hinds Mfg.
300 Wildwood Ave.
Woburn, MA 01801
(800) 874-4788
www.catherinehinds.com

DNR CA Botana Int'l, Inc.
9365 Waples St., Ste. A
San Diego, CA 92121
(800) 872-2332; (858) 450-1717
www.ca-botana.com

◆ Cacharel
(see L'Oreal)

▼ Calgon
(see Reckitt-Benckiser plc)

◆ California Baby Botanical Skin Care ■
217 S. Linden Dr.
Beverly Hills, CA 90212-3704
(877) 576-2825; (310) 277-6430
www.californiababy.com
Personal Care

◆ California Gold products
(see J & J Jojoba)

DNR California Mango
17712 Crabb Ln.
Huntington Beach, CA 92647-6707
(714) 375-2599

▼ Calvin Klein fragrances
(see Unilever)

▼ Camay
(see Procter & Gamble)

▼ Cameo Cleaner
(see Church & Dwight Co., Inc.)

DNR Camille Beckman
P.O. Box 2820
Boise, ID 83701
(208) 386-9196
www.camillebeckman.com

▼ Carefree
(see Johnson & Johnson)

▼ Caress
(see Unilever)

♥ Carma Laboratories, Inc. ■
5801 W. Airways Ave.
Franklin, WI 53132
(414) 421-7707
www.carma-labs.com
Personal Care

♥ Carmex Lip Balm
(see Carma Laboratories, Inc.)

▼ Cascade
(see Procter & Gamble)

DNR Cassini Parfums, Ltd.
3 W. 57th St., 8th Fl.
New York, NY 10019
(212) 755-3490

DNR Caswell-Massey Co. Ltd.
121 Fieldcrest Ave.
Edison, NJ 08837
(732) 225-2181
www.caswellmassey.com

◆ Cat's Pride cat litter
(see Oil-Dri Corp. of America)

▼ Caudalle ■
9 Villa Aublet
75017 Paris France
(214) 826-1615 X222
www.caudalie.com
Cosmetics

DNR CCA Industries, Inc.
200 Murray Hill Pkwy.
East Rutherford, NJ 07073
(201) 935-3232; (201) 330-1400
www.ccaindustries.com

◆ CD&P Health Products, Inc. ■
86 Lackawanna Ave., Ste. 318
West Paterson, NJ 07424
(800) 922-0164
www.floraspa.com
Personal Care

♥ Celebrate fragrance
(see Marilyn Miglin, L.P.)

DNR Celestial Body
21298 Pleasant Hill Rd.
Boonville, MO 65233
(800) 882-6858
www.celestialbody.com

♥ Ceramide
(see Elizabeth Arden, Inc.)

▼ Cerruti fragrances
(see Unilever)

♥ Chanel, Inc. ■
9 W. 57th St.
New York, NY 10019
(800) 550-0005; (212) 688-5055
www.chanel.com
Cosmetics, Personal Care

DNR Change of Face Cosmetics
P.O. Box 592
Hobart, IN 46342
(800) 865-1755; (219) 947-4040

♥ Charlie
(see Revlon, Inc.)

▼ Charmin
(see Procter & Gamble)

DNR Chattem, Inc.
1715 W. 38th St.
Chattanooga, TN 37409
(800) 366-6077; (423) 821-4571
www.chattem.com

▼ Cheer
(see Procter & Gamble)

DNR Cherry Vanilla
(see CCA Industries, Inc.)

❤ Chishti Co. ■
P.O. Box 12039
Tucson, AZ 85732
(800) 344-7172; (520) 296-6900
www.chishti.com
Personal Care

▼ Chloe
(see Unilever)

DNR Cholesterol
(see Para Laboratories, Inc.)

DNR Christian Dior fragrances
(see LVMH Moet Hennessy Louis
Vuitton)

◆ Christine Valmy ■
285 Change Bridge Rd.
Pine Brook, NJ 07058
(800) 526-5057; (973) 575-1050
www.christinevalmy.com
Personal Care

DNR Chuckles, Inc.
P.O. Box 5126
Manchester, NH 03108-5126
(800) 221-3496; (603) 669-4228

▼ Church & Dwight Co., Inc. ■
P.O. Box 1625
Horsham, PA 19044-6625
(800) 524-1328; (609) 683-5900
www.churchdwight.com
*Companion Animal Care, Household,
Personal Care*

❤ CiCi Cosmetics ■
215 N. Eucalyptus Ave.
Inglewood, CA 90301
(800) 869-1224; (310) 680-9696
www.cicicosmetics.com
Cosmetics

DNR Cinema Secrets by Maurice Stein
4400 Riverside Dr.
Burbank, CA 91505
(818) 846-0579
www.cinemasecrets.com

◆ Citra-Clear
(see Citra-Solv, LLC)

- ◆ Citra-Dish
  (see Citra-Solv, LLC)

- ◆ Citra-Drain
  (see Citra-Solv, LLC)

- DNR Citra-Glow
  (see Mia Rose Products, Inc.)

- ◆ Citra-Solv
  (see Citra-Solv, LLC)

- ◆ Citra-Solv, LLC ✳ ■
  P.O. Box 2597
  Danbury, CT 06813-2597
  (800) 343-6588; (203) 778-0881
  www.citra-solv.com
  Household, Personal Care

- ◆ Citra-Spot
  (see Citra-Solv, LLC)

- ◆ Citra-Suds
  (see Citra-Solv, LLC)

- ◆ Citra-Wood
  (see Citra-Solv, LLC)

- DNR Citre Shine
  (see Advanced Research Laboratories)

- ▼ Citrucel
  (see GlaxoSmithKline Consumer
  Healthcare)

- DNR Citrus Magic products
  (see Beaumont Products, Inc.)

- DNR Claire Burke
  (see Esscentual Brands, LLC)

- ▼ Clairol
  (see Procter & Gamble)

- DNR Clarins USA Inc.
  110 E. 59th St.
  New York, NY 10022
  (212) 980-1800
  www.clarins.com

- DNR Classic Cosmetics, Inc.
  9601 Irondale Ave.
  Chatsworth, CA 91311
  (818) 773-9042
  www.classiccosmetics.com

- ▼ Clean & Clear
  (see Johnson & Johnson)

◆ Clean & Easy ■
2220 Gaspar Ave.
Los Angeles, CA 90040
(323) 728-2999
www.aiibeauty.com
Cosmetics, Personal Care
(see American Int'l Ind.)

▼ Clean Burst
(see Personal Products Co.)

◆ Clean Shine
(see USA Detergents)

▼ Clean Shower
(see Church & Dwight Co., Inc.)

❤ Clear Conscience, LLC ✳ ■ ▣
P.O. Box 17855
Arlington, VA 22216
(800) 595-9592; (703) 527-7566
www.clearconscience.com
Personal Care

◆ Clear Light The Cedar Co. ■
Box 551
Placitas, NM 87043
(800) 557-3463; (505) 867-2381
www.clcedar.com
Personal Care

DNR Clear Logix
(see Advanced Research Laboratories)

❤ Clearly Natural Products ✳ ■
1340 N. McDowell Blvd.
Petaluma, CA 94975-0024
(800) 274-7627; (707) 762-5815
www.clearlynaturalsoaps.com
Personal Care

DNR Clientele
14101 N.W. Fourth St.
Sunrise, FL 33325-6209
(954) 845-9500
www.clientele.org

❤ Clinique
(see Estee Lauder Companies)

▼ Clorox Co. ■
1221 Broadway
Oakland, CA 94612
(510) 271-7000
www.thecloroxcompany.com
*Companion Animal Care, Household,
Personal Care*

▼ Clorox products
(see Clorox Co.)

▼ Close-Up
(see Church & Dwight Co., Inc.)

DNR CLR
(see Jelmar, Inc.)

◆ Clubman ■
2220 Gaspar Ave.
Los Angeles, CA 90040
(323) 728-2999
www.aiibeauty.com
Cosmetics, Personal Care
(see American Int'l Ind.)

▼ Coast
(see Dial Corp., Inc.)

DNR Cold Wax Co.
P.O. Box 600476
San Diego, CA 92160
(619) 283-0880

▼ Colgate products
(see Colgate-Palmolive Co.)

▼ Colgate-Palmolive Co. ■
300 Park Ave.
New York, NY 10022-7499
(800) 221-4607; (212) 310-2000
www.colgate.com
*Companion Animal Care, Household,
Personal Care*

DNR Colin Ingram Co.
P.O. Box 146
Comptche, CA 95427-0146
(707) 937-4971
www.coliningram.com

DNR Colonial Dames Co. Ltd.
P.O. Box 22022
Los Angeles, CA 90022
(800) 774-6441; (213) 773-6441
www.colonial-dames.com

DNR Color Me Beautiful, Inc.
14900 Conference Center Dr.
Chantilly, VA 20151
(800) COLORME; (703) 471-6400
www.colormebeautiful.com

❤ Color My Image Inc. ✳ ▫
5025B Backlick Rd.
Annadale, VA 22003
(703) 354-9797
www.colormyimage.com
Cosmetics

◆ Colora Henna ✳ ■
217 Washington Ave.
Carlstadt, NJ 07072
(201) 939-0969
Cosmetics

DNR Colour Energy Corp.
758 Powell St.
Vancouver, BC, V6A 1H6, Canada
(800) 225-1226; (604) 687-3757
www.colourenergy.com

DNR Columbia Cosmetics
1661 Timothy Dr.
San Leandro, CA 94577
(510) 562-5900
www.columbiacosmetics.com

▼ Combat
(see Clorox Co.)

DNR Concept Now Cosmetics
P.O. Box 3208
Santa Fe Springs, CA 90670
(562) 903-1450
www.conceptnowcosmetics.com

◆ Connie Stevens/Forever Spring ✳ ▫
426 S. Robertson
Los Angeles, CA 90048
(310) 657-5910
www.foreverspring.com
Cosmetics, Personal Care

DNR Consolidated Ecoprogress
Technology, Inc.
885 Dunsmuir St., Ste. 910
Vancouver, BC, Canada
Canada V6C 1N5
(604) 738-7011
www.flushaway.com

❤ Consort
(see Alberto Culver)

DNR Copper Brite Inc.
P.O. Box 50610
Santa Barbara, CA 93150-0610
(805) 565-1566
www.copperbrite.com

▼ Coppertone
(see Schering-Plough Corp.)

DNR Corn Huskers lotion
(see Pfizer)

▼ CornSilk
(see Del Laboratories, Inc.)

DNR Cosmetic Group, U.S.A.
11340 Penrose St.
Sun Valley, CA 91352
(818) 767-2889

DNR Cot'n Wash, Inc.
502 The Times Bldg.
Ardmore, PA 19003
(800) 355-WASH; (610) 896-4372

▼ Cottonelle
(see Kimberly-Clark Corp.)

◆ Country Air
(see USA Detergents)

DNR Country Comfort
P.O. Box 2716
Lake Arrowhead, CA 92352
(610) 896-4378

◆ Country Save Corp. ❄■
19704 60th Ave. NE
Arlington, WA 98223
(360) 435-9868
www.countrysave.com
Household

▼ Cover Girl
(see Procter & Gamble)

DNR CoverBlend
(see NeoStrata Co.)

DNR Covermark Cosmetics
157 Veterans Dr.
Northvale, NJ 07647-2301
(201) 460-7713
www.covermark.com

DNR CPAC, Inc.
2364 Leicester Rd.
Leicester NY 14481
(800) 828-6011; (585) 382-3223
www.cpac-fuller.com

▼ Crest
(see Procter & Gamble)

◆ Crystal Body Deodorant
(see French Transit)

▼ Crystal Clean
(see Colgate-Palmolive Co.)

◆ Crystal Shine
(see USA Detergents)

▼ Crystal White Octagon
(see Colgate-Palmolive Co.)

◆ Curad
(see Beiersdorf, Inc.)

◆ Curél products
(see Kao Brands Co. (formerly
Andrew Jergens Co.))

▼ Custom Plus
(see Gillette Co.)

DNR Cutex Co.
488 Main Ave.
Norwalk, CT 06851
www.cutexnails.com

▼ Daily Defense
(see Procter & Gamble)

▼ Daisy
(see Gillette Co.)

DNR Danklied Laboratories, Ltd.
P.O. Box 436
Cazenovia, NY 13035
(800)497-4757
www.danklied.com

♥ Darphin
(see Estee Lauder Companies)

▼ Dawn
(see Procter & Gamble)

DNR Decleor USA Inc.
100 Tokeneke Rd.
Darien, CT 06820
(888) 414-447
www.decleor.com

▼ Degree
(see Unilever)

▼ Del Laboratories, Inc. ■
565 Broad Hollow Rd.
Farmingdale, NY 11735
(800) 952-5080; (516) 844-2020
www.dellabs.com
Cosmetics, Personal Care

▼ Delicare
(see Church & Dwight Co., Inc.)

- ◆ Delore ■
  2220 Gaspar Ave.
  Los Angeles, CA 90040
  (323) 728-2999
  www.aiibeauty.com
  Cosmetics, Personal Care
  (see American Int'l Ind.)

- ◆ Dena Corp. ✳ ■
  850 Nicholas Blvd.
  Elk Grove Village, IL 60007
  (847) 593-3041
  www.denacorp.com
  Personal Care

- ◆ Dena Vie
  (see Dena Corp.)

- DNR Den-Mat Corp.
  2727 Skyway Dr.
  Santa Maria, CA 93455
  (800) 548-3663
  www.denmat.com

- ◆ Deodorant Stones of America ✳ ■
  9420 E. Doubletree Ranch Rd.,
  # C101
  Scottsdale, AZ 85258
  (800) 279-9318; (480) 451-4981
  www.deodorantstones.com
  Personal Care

- ▼ Dep
  (see Schwarzkopf & Dep Inc.)

- ▼ Depend
  (see Kimberly-Clark Corp.)

- ❤ Derma E ✳ ■
  4485 Runway St.
  Simi Valley, CA 93063
  (800) 521-3342
  www.dermae.net
  Personal Care

- ◆ Dermablend
  (see L'Oreal)

- DNR Derma-Life Corp.
  706 Foothill Ct.
  Boulder City, NV 89005
  (505) 888-1789

♥ Dermalogica, Inc. ■
1001 Knox St.
Torrance, CA 90502
(800) 831-5150; (310) 436-3408
www.dermalogica.com
Personal Care

▼ Dermassage
(see Colgate-Palmolive Co.)

DNR Dermatologic Cosmetic Laboratories
20 Commerce St.
East Haven, CT 06512
(800) 552-5060; (203) 467-1570
www.dclskincare.com

DNR Dermatone Labs Inc.
80 King Spring Rd.
Windsor Locks, CT 06096
(800) 225-7546
www.dermatone.com

DNR Desert Essence
27460 Ave. Scott
Valencia, CA 91355-3473
(516) 232-5472
www.desertessence.com

♥ Design
(see Elizabeth Arden, Inc.)

DNR Desitin
(see Pfizer)

DNR Desoto LLC
P.O. Box 609
Joliet, IL 60434-0609
(815) 727-4931

♥ Destiny fragrance
(see Marilyn Miglin, L.P.)

▼ Dial Corp., Inc. ■
15501 N. Dial Blvd.
Scottsdale, AZ 85260-1619
(800) 258-DIAL; (480) 754-3425
www.dialcorp.com
Household, Personal Care
(see Henkel KGaA)

▼ Dial products
(see Dial Corp., Inc.)

◆ Dickinson Brands Inc. ✳ ■ ⊡
31 E. High St.
East Hampton, CT 06424
(888) 860-2279; (860) 267-2279
www.witchhazel.com
Cosmetics, Personal Care

- ◆ Dickinson's
  (see Dickinson Brands Inc.)

- DNR Dionis Inc.
  P.O. Box 5142
  Charlottesville, VA 22905
  (800) 566-7627
  www.dionissoap.com

- DNR Discount Deodorant Stones
  3503 Vara Dr.
  Austin, TX 78754-4928
  (800) 926-5233; (512) 926-9662

- ❤ Divine fragrance
  (see Marilyn Miglin, L.P.)

- ▼ Dixie
  (see Georgia-Pacific)

- ❤ Dog Poo
  (see Sunfeather Natural Soap Co.)

- ❤ Donna Karan Cosmetics
  (see Estee Lauder Companies)

- ▼ Dove
  (see Unilever)

- ▼ Downy
  (see Procter & Gamble)

- DNR Dr. A. C. Daniels
  109 Worcester Rd.
  Webster, MA 01570-2102
  (800) 547-3760; (508) 943-5563
  www.drdaniels.com

- ❤ Dr. Bronner's Magic Soaps ✳ ■
  P.O. Box 28
  Escondido, CA 92033
  (760) 743-2211
  www.drbronner.com
  Household, Personal Care

- ❤ Dr. Goodpet ■
  P.O. Box 4547
  Inglewood, CA 90309
  (800) 222-9932
  www.goodpet.com
  Companion Animal Care

- DNR Dr. Grandel
  32496 U.S. Hwy. 281 N.
  Bulverde, TX 78613
  (800) 543-5230
  www.grandelusa.com

❤ Dr. Hauschka Skin Care, Inc. ■
59 North St.
Hatfield, MA 01038
(413) 247-9907
www.drhauschka.com
Cosmetics, Personal Care

▼ Dr. Scholl's
(see Schering-Plough Corp.)

DNR Dr. Singhas Natural Therapeutics
2500 Side Cove
Austin, TX 78704
(512) 444-2862
www.drsingha.com

▼ Drano
(see S.C. Johnson)

DNR Dreamous Corp.
12016 Wilshire Blvd.
Los Angeles, CA 90025
(800) 251-7543; (310) 442-8544
www.dreamous.com

▼ Dreft
(see Procter & Gamble)

▼ Dry Idea
(see Gillette Co.)

▼ Dryel
(see Procter & Gamble)

▼ Duracell
(see Gillette Co.)

▼ Dynamo
(see Colgate-Palmolive Co.)

DNR E.P.T. Early Pregnancy Test
(see Pfizer)

❤ Earth Essentials ■
P.O. Box 40339
Santa Barbara, CA 93140-0339
(800) 347-5211; (805) 684-4525
www.earthessentials.com
Cosmetics, Household, Personal Care

DNR Earth Friendly Baby
P.O. Box 400
Charlotte, VT 05445
(802) 425-4300
www.earthfriendlybaby.com

❤ Earth Friendly Products ❋ ■
44 Green Bay Rd.
Winnetka, IL 60093
(800) 335-ECOS; (847) 446-4441
www.ecos.com
Household

DNR Earth Science, Inc.
475 N. Sheridan
Corona, CA 91720
(800) 222-6720; (909) 371-7505
www.earthscienceinc.com

DNR Earth Secrets
(see Luster Products, Inc.)

DNR Earth Solutions, Inc.
1123 Zonolite, Ste. 8
Atlanta, GA 30306
(800) 883-3376; (404)525-6167
www.earthsolutions.com

❤ Earthly Matters ❋ ■ ▫
2950 St. Augustine Rd.
Jacksonville, FL 32207
(904) 398-1458
Household

◆ Earthsafe products
(see NAACO)

❤ earthscience
(see Earth Essentials)

▼ Easy-Off
(see Reckitt-Benckiser plc)

DNR EB5 Corp.
2711 NW Saint Helens Rd.
Portland, OR 97210
(503) 230-8008
www.eb5.com

DNR Ecco Bella
1133 Rte. 23 South
Wayne, NJ 07470
(877) 696-2220; (973) 696-7766
www.eccobella.com

❤ Eco-Dent Int'l, Inc. ❋ ■
P.O. Box 325
Twin Lakes, WI 53181-0325
(262) 889-8561
www.eco-dent.com
Personal Care

◆ Ecover Int'l ■
P.O. Box 911058
Commerce, CA 90091-1058
(800) 449-4925; (323) 720-5730
www.ecover.com
Household

❤ Eden Botanicals ■
P.O. Box 150
Hyampom, CA 96046
(530) 628-5612
www.edenbotanicals.com
Personal Care

▼ Edge
(see S.C. Johnson)

DNR Efferdent
(see Pfizer)

▼ Electrasol
(see Reckitt-Benckiser plc)

❤ Elizabeth Arden 5th Avenue
(see Elizabeth Arden, Inc.)

❤ Elizabeth Arden Green Tea
(see Elizabeth Arden, Inc.)

❤ Elizabeth Arden Provocative Woman
(see Elizabeth Arden, Inc.)

❤ Elizabeth Arden, Inc. ■
200 First Stamford Pl.
Stamford, CT 06902
(800) 326-7337; (203) 462-5700
www.elizabetharden.com
Cosmetics, Personal Care

❤ Elizabeth Arden's Red Door
(see Elizabeth Arden, Inc.)

❤ Elizabeth Taylor's Passion
(see Elizabeth Arden, Inc.)

❤ Elizabeth Taylor's White Diamonds
(see Elizabeth Arden, Inc.)

❤ Elizabeth Van Buren Inc. ✳ ■
303 Potrero St., Ste. 33
Santa Cruz, CA 95060-2756
(831) 425-8218
www.evb-aromatherapy.com
Cosmetics, Personal Care

DNR Ellegance
(see NaturElle Cosmetics Corp.)

◆ Elysee Scientific Cosmetics ■
203 Legion St.
Verona, WI 53593
(800) 235-9733; (608) 271-3664
www.elyseecosmetics.com
Cosmetics, Personal Care

◆ Eqyss Int'l ✳ ■
P.O. Box 130008
Carlsbad, CA 92013-0008
(800) 526-7469
www.eqyss.com
*Companion Animal Care,
Personal Care*

▼ Era
(see Procter & Gamble)

❤ Espree Animal Products, Inc. ✳ ■
637 Westport Pkwy., Ste. 208
Grapevine, TX 76051
(800) 328-1317
www.espree.com
Companion Animal Care

DNR Esscentual Brands, LLC
4835 E. Cactus Rd., Ste. 245
Scottsdale, AZ 85254
(602) 889-4800
www.esscentualbrands.com

❤ Essential 3 (formerly Jacki's
Magic Lotion) ■ ▣
145 Hummingbird Ln.
Talent, OR 97540
(800) 355-8428; (541) 535-1866
www.meadowsusa.com
Personal Care

DNR Essentially Yours Industries Corp.
4295 Ensenada Dr.
Woodland Hills, CA 91364
(818) 340-3199
www.eyicom.com

❤ Estee Lauder Companies ■
767 Fifth Ave.
New York, NY 10153
(212) 572-4200
www.elcompanies.com
Cosmetics, Personal Care

◆ Eucerin
(see Beiersdorf, Inc.)

▼ Eukanuba
(see The Iams Company)

◆ European Mystique
(see Dena Corp.)

◆ European Secrets ■
2220 Gaspar Ave.
Los Angeles, CA 90040
(323) 728-2999
www.aiibeauty.com
Cosmetics, Personal Care
(see American Int'l Ind.)

DNR European Soaps, Ltd.
920 N. 137th St.
Seattle, WA 98133-7505
(800) 426-9260
www.europeansoaps.com

DNR Eva Jon Cosmetics
1016 E. California St.
Gainesville, TX 76240
(940) 668-7707

▼ EverClean
(see Clorox Co.)

▼ EverFresh
(see Clorox Co.)

DNR Everybody Ltd.
1738 Pearl St.
Boulder, CO 80302
(800) 748-5675; (303) 440-0188
www.everybodyltd.com

◆ Exotic Nature Body Care Products ■
2535 Village Ln., Ste. E
Cambria, CA 93428-3428
(805) 927-2517
www.exoticnature.com
Personal Care

DNR Exuviance
(see NeoStrata Co.)

▼ Fa body washes
(see Schwarzkopf & Dep Inc.)

▼ Fab products
(see Colgate-Palmolive Co.)

◆ Fabulous
(see USA Detergents)

DNR Face to Face
20861 Ventura Blvd.
Woodland Hills, CA 91364-2319
(818) 888-1817

DNR Fantasia Industries, Inc.
20 Park Pl.
Paramus, NJ 07652-3617
(201) 261-7070
www.fantasiahaircare.com

▼ Fantastik
(see S.C. Johnson)

DNR Fashion Fair Cosmetics
820 S. Michigan
Chicago, IL 60605
(312) 322-9444
www.fashionfaircosmetics.com

DNR Faultless Starch
1025 W. 8th St.
Kansas City, MO 64101
(816) 842-1230
www.bonami.com

❤ FDS
(see Alberto Culver)

▼ Febreze
(see Procter & Gamble)

▼ Fels Naptha
(see Dial Corp., Inc.)

▼ Final Touch
(see Unilever)

◆ Fine Care
(see USA Detergents)

DNR Finelle Cosmetics
12907 Medford Rd.
Philadelphia, PA 19154
(800) 956-5652
www.finelle.com

▼ Finesse
(see Unilever)

❤ Fire & Ice fragrance
(see Revlon, Inc.)

DNR Firoze Nail & Skin Care
400 E. 71 St., Ste. 11T
New York, NY 10021
(212) 249-5445
www.firoze.com

▼ First Response
(see Church & Dwight Co., Inc.)

DNR Five Star Fragrance Co.
1095 Long Island Ave.
Deer Park, NY 11729
(631) 254-9330
www.qkd.com

▼ Fixodent
(see Procter & Gamble)

❤ Fleabusters/Rx for Fleas, Inc. ✳ ■ ▨
6555 NW 9th Ave., Ste. 412
Fort Lauderdale, FL 33309
(800) 666-3532; (305) 351-9244
www.fleabuster.com
Companion Animal Care, Household

❤ Flee Flea Oil
(see Sunfeather Natural Soap Co.)

❤ Flex
(see Revlon, Inc.)

DNR Flicker
(see American Safety Razor Co.)

DNR Flori Roberts
(see Color Me Beautiful, Inc.)

DNR Flower Essence Services
P.O. Box 1769
Nevada City, CA 95959
(800) 548-0075, (916) 265-0258
www.floweressence.com

DNR Flowery Beauty Products
107 Mill Plain Rd., Ste. 303
Danbury, CT 06811
(800) 545-5247; (203) 205-0686
www.flowery.com

DNR Footherapy
(see Para Laboratories, Inc.)

DNR Forest Essentials
601 Del Norte Blvd., Ste. F
Oxnard, CA 93030-8981
(805) 278-8975
www.forestessentials.com

❤ Forever Elizabeth
(see Elizabeth Arden, Inc.)

◆ Forever New Int'l, Inc. ✳ ■
4701 N. Fourth Ave.
Sioux Falls, SD 57104-0403
(800) 456-0107; (605) 331-2910
www.forevernew.com
Household, Personal Care

▼ Formula 409
(see Clorox Co.)

DNR Four Elements Herbals
E. 8984 Weinke Rd.
North Freedom, WI 53951
(608) 522-4492
www.naturesacres-herbals.com

◆ Framesi USA ✳ ■
400 Chess St.
Coraopolis, PA 15108
(412) 269-2950
www.framesi.it
Cosmetics, Personal Care

DNR Frances Denney
4829 E. Broadway Ave.
Tampa, FL 33605
(800) 6-DENNEY
www.francesdenney.com

❤ Frank T. Ross & Sons, Ltd. ✳ ■
6550 Lawrence Ave.
Toronto, Ontario, Canada M1C 4A7
(416) 282-1107
www.franktross.com
Household, Personal Care

DNR Frederic Fekkai & Co.
600 Madison Ave.
New York, NY 10022

❤ Freeman Beauty ■
10474 Santa Monica Blvd., Ste. 300
Beverly Hills, CA 90213
(310) 446-9300
www.freemanbeauty.com
Personal Care

◆ French Transit ✳ ■
398 Beach Rd.
Burlingame, CA 94010
(800) 829-ROCK; (650) 548-9600
www.thecrystal.com
Personal Care

DNR Fresh
(see LVMH Moet Hennessy Louis
Vuitton)

DNR Fresh 'N Brite toothpaste
(see Pfizer)

▼ Fresh Step
(see Clorox Co.)

▼ Fresh'n Clean
(see Church & Dwight Co., Inc.)

◆ Frizz Ender
(see Dena Corp.)

◆ Frizz-Ease
(see Kao Brands Co. (formerly
Andrew Jergens Co.))

▼ Frost & Tip
(see Procter & Gamble)

DNR Fruit of the Earth, Inc.
2520 W. Irving Blvd., Ste. 300
Irving, TX 75061
(800) 527-7731; (972) 790-0808
www.fote.com

DNR Fuller Brush Co.
One Fuller Way
Great Bend, KS 67530
(620) 792-1711
www.fuller.com
(see CPAC, Inc.)

▼ Future
(see S.C. Johnson)

❤ Gabriel Cosmetics, Inc. ■
P.O. Box 50130
Bellevue, WA 98105
(425) 885-9800
www.gabrielcosmeticsinc.com
Cosmetics, Personal Care

DNR Gaiam Inc.
360 Interlocken Blvd., Ste. 300
Broomfield, CO 80021
(800) 869-3446
www.gaiam.com

▼ Gain
(see Procter & Gamble)

DNR Gale Hayman fragrance
(see Color Me Beautiful, Inc.)

◆ Gannon's, Inc. ✳ ■ ▣
P.O. Box 345
Portsmouth, OH 45662-0345
(740) 353-1667
www.odorbgoneproducts.com
Companion Animal Care, Household

DNR Gap fragrances
(see Gap, Inc.)

DNR Gap, Inc.
One Harrison St.
San Francisco, CA 94105
(800) 333-7899; (650) 952-4400
www.gapinc.com

❤ Garden Botanika ■
11121 Willows Rd., Ste. 210
Redmond, WA 98052
(800) 968-7842; (425) 896-4467
www.gardenbotanika.com
Cosmetics, Personal Care
(see Schroeder & Tremayne, Inc.)

♥ Gardenia
(see Elizabeth Arden, Inc.)

◆ Garnier
(see L'Oreal)

DNR GEM
(see American Safety Razor Co.)

◆ Gena Laboratories ■
2220 Gaspar Ave.
Los Angeles, CA 90040
(323) 728-2999
www.aiibeauty.com
Cosmetics, Personal Care
(see American Int'l Ind.)

▼ Gentle Naturals
(see Del Laboratories, Inc.)

♥ Geoffrey Beene Grey Flannel
(see Elizabeth Arden, Inc.)

◆ Georgette Klinger Inc. ✳ ■ ▨
501 Madison Ave.
New York, NY 10022
(212) 838-3200
www.georgetteklinger.com
Cosmetics, Personal Care

▼ Georgia-Pacific ■
133 Peachtree St., N.E
Atlanta, GA 30303
(800) 519-3111; (404) 652-4000
www.gp.com
Household

♥ Gerda Spillmann USA ■ ▨
640 Glass Ln.
Modesto, CA 95356
(209) 529-1757
www.gerdaspillmann.com
Cosmetics, Personal Care

◆ Gigi Laboratories ■
2220 Gaspar Ave.
Los Angeles, CA 90040
(323) 728-2999
www.aiibeauty.com
Cosmetics, Personal Care
(see American Int'l Ind.)

▼ Gillette Co. ■
Prudential Tower Bldg., Ste. 4800
Boston, MA 02199
(800) 872-7202; (617) 421-7000
www.gillette.com
Personal Care

▼ Gillette products
(see Gillette Co.)

◆ Giorgio Armani Parfums
(see L'Oreal)

▼ Giorgio Beverly Hills
(see Procter & Gamble)

DNR Giovanni Hair Care Products
P.O. Box 39378
Los Angeles, CA 90039
(310) 952-9960
www.giovannicosmetics.com

DNR Givenchy fragrances
(see LVMH Moet Hennessy Louis
Vuitton)

▼ Glad products
(see Clorox Co.)

DNR Glad Rags
(see Keepers! Inc.)

▼ Glade products
(see S.C. Johnson)

▼ GladWare
(see Clorox Co.)

DNR Glass Glo
(see Pine Glo Products, Inc.)

▼ GlaxoSmithKline
Consumer Healthcare ■
P.O. Box 1467
Pittsburgh, PA 15230
(800) 456-6670; (412) 200-4000
www.gsk.com
Personal Care

♥ Glean Kids Naturally
(see Gabriel Cosmetics, Inc.)

▼ Gleem
(see Procter & Gamble)

DNR Global Health Alternatives
2161 Hutton Dr., Ste. 126
Carrollton, TX 75006-8333
(800) 4BE-CALM

DNR Glo-Marr Products, Inc.
400 Lincoln St.
Lawrenceburg, KY 40342-1282
(800) 228-7387; (502) 839-6996
www.glo-marr-kenic.com

DNR Gly-Miracle
(see Progressive Beauty Brands)

DNR Glysolid
(see Sara Lee Corp.)

❤ Goddess fragrance
(see Marilyn Miglin, L.P.)

DNR Gold Bond
(see Chattem, Inc.)

DNR Gold Medal Hair Products, Inc.
One Bennington Ave.
Freeport, NY 11520
(800) 535-8101; (516) 378-6900
www.goldmedalhair.com

DNR Goldwell Cosmetics Inc.
981 Corporate Blvd.
Linthicum Heights, MD 21090
(800) 288-9118; (410) 850-7555
www.goldwellusa.com

▼ Good News
(see Gillette Co.)

▼ Good Nites
(see Kimberly-Clark Corp.)

◆ Goodier Cosmetics ■
9027 Diplomacy Row
Dallas, TX 75247-5303
(214) 630-1803
www.goodiercosmetics.com
Cosmetics, Personal Care

DNR got2b
(see Advanced Research Laboratories)

▼ Grab-it
(see S.C. Johnson)

❧ Graham Webb ■
5823 Newton Dr.
Carlsbad, CA 92008
(800) 470-9909 (760) 918-3600
www.backtobasics.com
Personal Care
(see Wella Corp.)

◆ Granny's Old Fashioned Products ■
1005 W. Foothill Blvd.
Azusa, CA 91702-2817
(626) 969-5066
www.gofproducts.com
Household, Personal Care

❤ Great Mother's Goods ✳ ■ ▣
P.O. Box 11425
Syracuse, NY 13218-1425
(800) 984-4848; (315) 476-1385
www.greatmothersgoods.com
Personal Care

DNR Green Ban
P.O. Box 146
Norway, IA 52318
(319) 446-7495
www.greenban.com

▼ Green Forest
(see Georgia-Pacific)

DNR Guerlain
(see LVMH Moet Hennessy Louis
Vuitton)

◆ Guhl
(see Kao Brands Co. (formerly
Andrew Jergens Co.))

DNR GUM
(see Sunstar Butler)

DNR H2O Plus, Inc.
845 W. Madison
Chicago, IL 60607
(800) 242-BATH; (312) 850-9283
www.h2oplus.com

DNR Hagen
50 Hampden Rd.
Mansfield, MA 02048
www.hagen.com

DNR Hair Doc Co.
16870 Stagg St.
Van Nuys, CA 91406
(800) 742-4736; (818) 989-4247

DNR Hair Off
(see CCA Industries, Inc.)

DNR Hair Therapy
(see Progressive Beauty Brands)

▼ Hairpainting
(see Procter & Gamble)

❤ Halston fragrance
(see Elizabeth Arden, Inc.)

❤ Halston Z-14
(see Elizabeth Arden, Inc.)

♥ Hard Candy ■
729 Farad St.
Costa Mesa, CA 92627
(949) 515-1250
www.hardcandy.com
Cosmetics

DNR Hawaiian Tropic products
(see Tanning Research Labs, Inc.)

♦ Hazelets
(see Dickinson Brands Inc.)

▼ Head & Shoulders
(see Procter & Gamble)

DNR Health and Body Fitness, Inc.
12021 Wilshire Blvd., Ste. 621
West Los Angeles, CA 90025
(562) 434-6417
healthandbodyfitness.com

DNR Health From The Sun
P.O. Box 360
Georges Mills, NH 03751-0360
(800) 447-2249

DNR Healthpoint, Ltd.
3909 Hulen St.
Fort Worth, Texas 76111
(800) 441-8227
www.healthpoint.com

♣ Healthy Defense
(see Neutrogena Corp.)

DNR Healthy Times
13200 Kirkham Way, #104
Poway, CA 92064-7115
(858) 513-1550

♦ Helena Rubenstein
(see L'Oreal)

▼ Helene Curtis
(see Unilever)

▼ Henkel KGaA ■
Henkelstrasse 67
40589 Dusseldorf, Germany
(49) 211 797 0
Household, Personal Care

DNR Henri Bendel, Inc.
712 5th Ave.
New York, NY 10019
(800) 423-6335; (212) 884-3000
www.henribendel.com
(see Limited, Inc.)

▼ Herbal Essences
(see Procter & Gamble)

DNR Herbal Logix
(see Advanced Research Laboratories)

DNR HerbaLife International
9800 La Cienega Blvd.
Englewood, CA 90301
(310) 410-9600
www.herbalife.com

DNR Heritage Store, Inc.
314 Laskin Rd.
Virginia Beach, VA 23451
(800) TO-CAYCE; (757) 428-0100
www.caycecures.com

DNR Hermes of Paris, Inc.
55 E. 59th St.
New York, NY 10022
(212) 759-7585
www.hermes.com

DNR Hewitt Soap Co., Inc.
333 Linden Ave.
Dayton, OH 45401
(800) 543-2245; (937) 253-1151
www.hewittsoap.com
(see Bradford Soap Works, Inc.)

➧ Hill's Pet Nutrition ■
P.O. Box 148
Topeka, KS 66601-0148
(800) 445-5777; (785) 354-8523
www.hillspet.com
Companion Animal Care
(see Colgate-Palmolive Co.)

▼ Hobe Laboratories, Inc. ■
6479 S. Ash Ave.
Tempe, AZ 85283-3657
(800) 528-4482
www.hobelabs.com
Personal Care

♥ Honeybee Gardens ■
1082 Palisades Dr.
Leesport, PA 19533-9395
(610) 396-9225
www.honeybeegardens.com
Cosmetics, Personal Care

DNR Horseman's Dream
P.O. Box 26797
Fort Worth, TX 76126
(817) 560-8818
www.horsemansdream.com

▼ Huggies
(see Kimberly-Clark Corp.)

▼ Hugo Boss fragrances
(see Procter & Gamble)

◆ Huish Detergents, Inc. ■
P.O. Box 25057
Salt Lake City, UT 84125
(800) 776-6702; (801) 975-3100
www.huish.com
Household

▼ Hydrience
(see Procter & Gamble)

DNR Hydron Technologies, Inc.
2201 W. Sample Rd., Ste. 9-5B
Pompano Beach, FL 33073-3006
(800) 449-3766
www.hydron.com

DNR Hygenic Cosmetics, Inc.
6500 NW Twelfth Ave. #114
Ft. Lauderdale, FL 33309
(800) 776-0555; (954) 491-0200

▼ Iams
(see The Iams Company)

DNR Icy Hot
(see Chattem, Inc.)

DNR ILONA, INC.
3201 E. Second Ave.
Denver, CO 80206
(303) 322-3000; (888) 38-ILONA
www.ilona.com

DNR Imageperfect
(see Jackie Brown Cosmetics)

DNR IMAN cosmetics
(see Color Me Beautiful, Inc.)

◆ Indigo Wild Aromatics ■ ⊡
3189 Mercer
Kansas City, MO 64111
(800) 361-5686; (816) 221-3480
www.indigowild.com
*Companion Animal Care,
Personal Care*

▼ Infusium 23
(see Procter & Gamble)

DNR Innovative Body Science
2724 Loker Ave. W
Carlsbad, CA 92008
(888) 700-7727
www.innovativebodyscience.com

DNR Institute of Trichology
13918 Equitable Rd.
Cerritos, CA 90703
(800) 458-8874; (562) 926-7373
www.trihaircare.com

DNR IPR 3
(see CCA Industries, Inc.)

▼ Irish Spring
(see Colgate-Palmolive Co.)

DNR Irving Tissue, Inc.
International Plz. 2, Ste. 405
Philadelphia, PA 19113
(800) 952-6633; (610) 362-0800
www.irvingtissue.com

◆ It's Organic Naturally
(see Dena Corp.)

▼ Ivory
(see Procter & Gamble)

▼ Ivory Snow
(see Procter & Gamble)

◆ J & J Jojoba
7826 Timm Rd.
Vacaville, CA 95688
(800) 380-6293; (707) 447-1207
www.californiagoldjojoba.com
Cosmetics, Personal Care

DNR Jackie Brown Cosmetics
5121 Gordon Smith Dr.
Rowlett, TX 75088
(800) 756-6138
www.imageperfect.com

DNR Jafra Cosmetics Int'l
2451 Townsgate Rd.
Westlake Village, CA 91361
(805) 449-3000
www.jafra.com

◆ James Austin Co. ✳ ■
P.O. Box 827
Mars, PA 16046-0827
(800) 245-1942; (412) 625-1535
www.jamesaustin.com
Household

DNR Jamieson Laboratories
2 St. Clair Ave. W, Ste. 1600
Toronto, Ontario, Canada M4V 1L5
(416) 960-0052
www.jamiesonvitamins.com

DNR Janet Sartin Cosmetics
500 Park Ave.
New York, NY 10022
(800) 321-1779; (212) 751-5858
www.sartin.com

❤ Jason Natural Products ■
3515 Eastham Dr.
Culver City, CA 90232
(877) JASON-01; (310) 838-7543
www.jason-natural.com
Cosmetics, Personal Care

❤ Jean Nate
(see Revlon, Inc.)

❤ Jeanne Gatineau
(see Revlon, Inc.)

❤ Jelene, Inc. ■
47 W. Maple Rd.
Clawson, MI 48017-1044
(248) 435-2446
Personal Care

DNR Jelmar, Inc.
5550 W. Touhy Ave., Ste. 2000
Skokie, IL 60077
(800) 323-5497; (847) 675-8400
www.jelmar.com

◆ Jergens products
(see Kao Brands Co. (formerly
Andrew Jergens Co.))

DNR Jessica McClintock
1400 Sixteenth St.
San Francisco, CA 94103
(800) 333-5301; (415) 495-3030
www.jessicamcclintock.com

▼ Jet-Dry
(see Reckitt-Benckiser plc)

❤ Jo Malone
(see Estee Lauder Companies)

◆ Joe Blasco Cosmetic Co. ■
1670 Hillhurst Ave.
Los Angeles, CA 90027-5580
(800) 553-1520
www.joeblasco.com
Cosmetics

DNR John Amico
4731 W. 136th St.
Crestwood, IL 60445-1968
(800) 676.5264; (708) 824-4000
www.johnamico.net

◆ John Frieda
(see Kao Brands Co. (formerly
Andrew Jergens Co.))

DNR John Paul Mitchell Systems
26455 Golden Valley Rd.
Saugus, CA 91350
(661) 298-0400
www.paulmitchell.com

▼ Johnson & Johnson ■
1 Johnson & Johnson Plz.
New Brunswick, NJ 08933-0001
(800) 635-6789; (732) 524-0400
www.jnj.com
Personal Care

▼ Johnson's Baby Oil
(see Johnson & Johnson)

▼ Johnson's Baby Powder
(see Johnson & Johnson)

◆ JOICO ■
100 Tokeneke Rd.
Darien, CT 06820
(800) 242-9283; (203) 655-8911
www.joico.com
Personal Care
(see Shiseido Cosmetics America)

◆ Jolen Creme Bleach Corp. ✳ ■
P.O. Box 458
Fairfield, CT 06430
(203) 259-8779
Personal Care

▼ Joy
(see Procter & Gamble)

♥ Jurlique Holistic Skin Corp. USA ■
2714 Apple Valley Rd., NE
Atlanta, GA 30319-3139
(404) 262-9382
www.jurlique.com
Personal Care

♥ Just for Me
(see Alberto Culver)

DNR Just for Redheads
8563 E San Alberto Dr., Ste. 135
Scottsdale, AZ 85258-4345
(800) 831-8240
www.justforredheads.com

DNR Just 'N Time stain remover
(see SerVaas Laboratories Inc.)

◆ Juvena
(see Beiersdorf, Inc.)

DNR Juvenesse by Elaine Gayle, Inc.
680 N. Lake Shore Dr.
Chicago, IL 60611
(312) 944-1211

◆ Kao Brands Co. (formerly Andrew
Jergens Co.) ■
P.O. Box 145444
Cincinnati, OH 45250-5444
(800) 742-8798; (513) 421-1400
www.kaobrands.com
Personal Care

♥ kate spade beauty
(see Estee Lauder Companies)

DNR Kaytee
521 Clay St., P.O. Box 230
Chilton, WI 53014
(800) 529-8331
www.kaytee.com

DNR Keepers! Inc.
P.O. Box 12648
Portland, OR 97212
(800) 799-4523
www.gladrags.com

DNR Kenra, Inc.
6501 Julian Ave.
Indianapolis, IN 46219
(317) 356-6491
www.kenra.com

DNR Kenzo fragrances
(see LVMH Moet Hennessy Louis
Vuitton)

◆ Kerastase
(see L'Oreal)

DNR Keri
(see Bristol-Myers Squibb Co.)

◆ Kettle Care ■ ▨
6590 Farm to Market Rd.
Whitefish, MT 59937-8301
(406) 862-9851
www.kettlecare.com
Personal Care

DNR Key West Aloe
524 Front St.
Key West, FL 33040
(800) 445-2563; (305) 294-5592
www.keywestaloe.com

◆ Kiehl's
(see L'Oreal)

DNR Kim Manley Herbals
P.O. Box 1266
Point Reyes Station, CA 94956
(707) 878-2980
www.kmherbals.com

▼ Kimberly-Clark Corp. ■
P.O. Box 2020
Neenah, WI 54957-2020
(800)665-9773
www.kimberly-clark.com
Household, Personal Care

❤ Kirk's Natural Products Corp. ✳ ■
7329 W. Harrison
Forest Park, IL 60130
(800) 825-4757; (708) 771-5475
www.kirksnatural.com
Personal Care

DNR Kiss My Face Corp.
P.O. Box 224
Gardiner, NY 12525-0224
(800) 262-KISS; (845) 255-0884
www.kissmyface.com

DNR Kiwi shoe care
(see Sara Lee Corp.)

▼ Kleenex
(see Kimberly-Clark Corp.)

◆ KMS Research LLC ■
P.O. Box 496040
Redding, CA 96049-6040
(800) DIALKMS; (530) 244-6000
www.kmshaircare.com
Personal Care

◆ Kneipp Corp. of America ■
105-107 Stonehurst Ct.
Northvale, NJ 07647-2405
(800) 937-4372; (201) 750-0600
www.kneipp.com
Personal Care

▼ Kotex
(see Kimberly-Clark Corp.)

DNR Kryolan Corp.
132 Ninth St.
San Francisco, CA 94103-2603
(800) Kryolan; (415) 863-9684
www.kryolan.com

◆ KSA Jojoba ✳ ■
19025 Parthenia St.
Northridge, CA 91324
(818) 701-1534
www.jojoba-ksa.com
*Companion Animal Care, Cosmetics,
Personal Care*

▼ K-Y Brand
(see Personal Products Co.)

DNR Kyjen Co.
P.O. Box 793
Huntington Beach, CA 92648
(800) 477-5735; (714) 704-1790
www.kyjen.com

▼ L.A. Looks
(see Schwarzkopf & Dep Inc.)

DNR La Crista, Inc.
P.O. Box 687
Frederick, MD 21701
(800) 888-2231
www.lacrista.com

DNR La Cross
565 Broad Hollow Rd.
Farmingdale, NY 11735
(631) 893-7529

▼ La Cross
(see Del Laboratories, Inc.)

DNR La Dove, Inc.
16100 NW 48th Ave.
Hialeah, FL 33014
(305) 624-2456
www.ladove.com

♥ La Mer
(see Estee Lauder Companies)

DNR La Natura
5033 Exposition Blvd.
Los Angeles, CA 90016
(800) 352-6288; (323) 766-0060
www.lanatura.com

▼ La Perla fragrance
(see Schwarzkopf & Dep Inc.)

◆ La Prairie
(see Beiersdorf, Inc.)

◆ La Roche-Posay
(see L'Oreal)

DNR Lady Burd
44 Executive Blvd.
Farmingdale, NY 11735
(631) 454-0444
www.ladyburd.com

▼ Lady Speed Stick
(see Colgate-Palmolive Co.)

▼ Lady's Choice
(see Church & Dwight Co., Inc.)

▼ Lagerfeld fragrances
(see Unilever)

♥ Lakon Herbals ■ ▣
720 Templeton Rd.
Montpelier, VT 05602-8584
(802) 223-5563
www.lakonherbals.com
Personal Care

▼ Lambert Kay
(see Church & Dwight Co., Inc.)

◆ Lancome
(see L'Oreal)

♥ Lanex Hemorrhoid Creme
(see Carma Laboratories, Inc.)

DNR L'anza Research Int'l
429 Santa Monica Blvd., Ste. 510
Santa Monica, CA 90401
(800) 423-0307
www.lanza.com

▼ Lasting Color
(see Procter & Gamble)

◆ Laundry Soft
(see USA Detergents)

DNR Laura Mercier
1000 Shiloh Rd., Ste. 200
Plano, TX 75074
(888) MERCIER; (713) 627-2050
www.lauramercier.com

DNR Lauren Amoresse Int'l
4981 Irwindale Ave.
Irwindale, CA 91706
(800) 258-7931
www.amoresse.com

▼ Lavoris
(see Schwarzkopf & Dep Inc.)

◆ Le Crystal Naturel
(see French Transit)

DNR Lee Pharmaceuticals
1434 Santa Anita Ave.
South El Monte, CA 91733
(800) 950-5337; (626) 442-3141
www.leepharmaceuticals.com

DNR Leslie Dee Ann Cosmetics
(see Neways Int'l)

▼ Lestoil
(see Clorox Co.)

▼ Lever 2000
(see Unilever)

▼ Lever Brothers
(see Unilever)

DNR Levlad, Inc./Nature's Gate
9200 Mason Ave.
Chatsworth, CA 91311
(800) 327-2012; (818) 882-2951
www.levlad.com

DNR Liberty Natural Products, Inc.
8120 S.E. Stark St.
Portland, OR 97215
(800) 289-8427; (503) 256-1227
www.libertynatural.com

▼ Lifebuoy
(see Unilever)

❤ Lifeline Co. ✳ ■
P.O. Box 531
Fairfax, CA 94978
(415) 457-9024
Household

❤ LifeTree
(see Earth Essentials)

▼ Lilt
(see Schwarzkopf & Dep Inc.)

DNR Lily of Colorado
P.O. Box 12471
Denver, CO 80212
(800) 333-5459; (303) 455-4194
www.lilyofcolorado.com

▼ Lime-A-Way
(see Reckitt-Benckiser plc)

DNR Limited Brands
3 Limited Pkwy.
Columbus, OH 43230-1467
(614) 415-7000
www.limitedbrands.com

◆ Linda Seidel ⊡
2328 W. Joppa Rd., Ste. 100
Lutherville, MD 21093-4668
(800) 752-0066; (410) 560-6999
www.lindaseidel.com
Cosmetics

❤ Lip Lube
(see Mad Gab's)

▼ Liquid-Plumr
(see Clorox Co.)

DNR Listerine
(see Pfizer)

DNR Listermint
(see Pfizer)

DNR Litter Purrfect
18595 Bernardo Trails Dr.
San Diego, CA 92128
(858) 451-3528

DNR Little Forest Natural Baby Products
501 Union St., Ste. 201
Nashville, TN 37219
(888) 329-BABY
www.littleforest.com

▼ Little Swimmers
(see Kimberly-Clark Corp.)

❤ Liz Claiborne Inc. ■
One Claiborne Ave.
North Bergen, NJ 07047
(201) 295-6000
www.lizclaiborne.com
Cosmetics

◆ Lobob Laboratories, Inc. ✳ ■
1440 Atteberry Ln.
San Jose, CA 95131-1410
(800) 835-6262; (408) 432-0580
www.loboblabs.com
Personal Care

DNR Lorac Cosmetics, Inc.
9559 Irondale Ave.
Chatsworth, CA 91311
(800) 845-0705
www.loraccosmetics.com

◆ L'Orbette ■
2220 Gaspar Ave.
Los Angeles, CA 90040
(323) 728-2999
www.aiibeauty.com
Cosmetics, Personal Care
(see American Int'l Ind.)

DNR Lord & Berry cosmetics
(see Markwins International Corp.
(formerly AM Cosmetics))

◆ L'Oreal ■
575 Fifth Ave.
New York, NY 10017
(800) 322-2036; (212) 818-1500
www.loreal.com
Cosmetics, Personal Care

◆ L'Oreal Paris
(see L'Oreal)

DNR Lotions & Potions
406 S. Rockford Dr., Ste. 6
Tempe, AZ 85281
(800) 462-7595; (480) 968-4662
www.lotionsandpotions.com

▼ Lotrimin
(see Schering-Plough Corp.)

❤ Louise Bianco Skin Care, Inc. ⊡
13655 Chandler Blvd.
Sherman Oaks, CA 91401
(800) 782-3067; (818) 786-2700
www.louisebianco.com
Cosmetics, Personal Care

▼ Loving Care
(see Procter & Gamble)

DNR Lubriderm
(see Pfizer)

❤ Lucky Chick ■
90 W. Dexter Plz.
Pearl River, NY 10965
(888) 920-0800
www.luckychick.com
Cosmetics, Personal Care

DNR Lucky Kentucky
(see Progressive Beauty Brands)

DNR Luster Products, Inc.
1104 W. 43rd St.
Chicago, IL 60609
(773) 579-1800
www.lusterproducts.com

DNR Lustrous Nails
(see Neways Int'l)

▼ Luvs
(see Procter & Gamble)

▼ Lux
(see Unilever)

◆ Luzier Cosmetics ■
7910 Troost Ave. # 2
Kansas City, MO 64131-1920
(816) 531-8338
www.luzier.com
Cosmetics, Personal Care

DNR LVMH Moet Hennessy Louis Vuitton
22 avenue Montaigne
75008 Paris France
(33) 1 44 13 22 22
www.lvmh.com

▼ Lysol
(see Reckitt-Benckiser plc)

❤ M for Men
(see Marilyn Miglin, L.P.)

❤ MAC
(see Estee Lauder Companies)

▼ MACH3 products
(see Gillette Co.)

♥ Mad Gab's ■
P.O. Box 426
Westbrook, ME 04098-0426
(207) 854-1679
www.madgabs.com
Personal Care

♥ Magic fragrance
(see Marilyn Miglin, L.P.)

♦ Magic of Aloe, Inc. ■ ⊡
7300 N. Crescent Blvd.
Pennsauken, NJ 08110
(800) 257-7770; (856) 662-3334
www.magicofaloe.com
Cosmetics, Personal Care

♥ Magick Botanicals ✳ ■
3412 W. MacArthur Blvd., Ste. K
Santa Ana, CA 92704
(800) 237-0674; (714) 957-0674
www.magickbotanicals.com
Personal Care

DNR Maharishi Ayur-Veda
Products Int'l Inc.
1068 Elkton Dr.
Colorado Springs, CO 80907
(800) 255-8332; (719) 260-5500
www.mapi.com

♦ Mallory Pet Supplies Inc. ■
740 Rankin Rd. NE
Albuquerque, NM 87107
(800) 824-4464; (505) 836-4033
Companion Animal Care

DNR Marae Storm
P.O. Box 203
Branscomb, CA 95417
(707) 984-8755

DNR Marcal Paper Mills, Inc.
1 Market St.
Elmwood Park, NJ 07407
(201) 796-4000
www.marcalpaper.com

♦ Marche Image Corp. ✳ ■
50 Webster Ave.
New Rochelle, NY 10801
(800) 753-9980; (914) 632-0165
Cosmetics, Personal Care

▼ Mardi Gras
(see Georgia-Pacific)

DNR Margarite Cosmetics
2138 Okeechobee Blvd.
West Palm Beach, FL 33409
(561) 686-1466

❤ Marilyn Miglin, L.P. ■ ▣
1230 W. Washington Blvd.
Chicago, IL 60607
(800) 322-1133
www.marilynmiglin.com
Cosmetics, Personal Care

DNR Mario Badescu Skin Care, Inc.
320 E. 52nd St.
New York, NY 10022
(800) BADESCU; (212) 758-1065
www.mariobadescu.com

DNR Markwins International Corp.
(formerly AM Cosmetics)
22067 Ferrero Pkwy.
City of Industry, CA 91789
(909) 595-8898
www.markwins.com

◆ Mary Ellen Products, Inc. ✳ ▣
P.O. Box 10
Grand Rapids, MN 55744
(218) 327-9989
www.maryellenproducts.com
Household

❤ Mary Kay Corp. ■ ▣
P.O. Box 799045
Dallas, TX 75379-9045
(800) 627-9529; (972) 687-5577
www.marykay.com
Cosmetics, Personal Care

▼ Massengill
(see GlaxoSmithKline Consumer
Healthcare)

❤ Master's Flower Essences ✳ ■
14618 Tyler Foote Rd.
Nevada City, CA 95959-9316
(800) 347-3639; (530) 478-7655
www.mastersessences.com
Personal Care

◆ Mastey De Paris, Inc. ■
25413 Rye Canyon Rd.
Valencia, CA 91355
(800) 6MASTEY; (661) 257-4814
www.mastey.com
Personal Care

◆ Matrix
(see L'Oreal)

◆ Mavala ■
1220 U.S. Hwy. 1, Ste. K
Palm Beach, FL 33408
(561) 624-9211
www.mavala-usa.com
Cosmetics

▼ Max Factor
(see Procter & Gamble)

◆ Maybelline
(see L'Oreal)

▼ MD
(see Georgia-Pacific)

DNR Medicine Flower
P.O. Box 385
Talent, OR 97540
(800) 787-9645; (541) 770-7051
www.medicineflower.com

DNR Mediclear
(see St. JON Laboratories)

♥ MediPatch Laboratories Corp. ✳ ■ ⬚
P.O. Box 795
E. Dennis, MA 02641
(508) 385-4549
www.holisticfamilyandpets.com
Companion Animal Care,
Personal Care

DNR Mega-G
(see CCA Industries, Inc.)

DNR Mehron, Inc.
100 Red Schoolhouse Rd.
Chestnut Ridge, NY 10977
(845) 426-1700
www.mehron.com

DNR Melaleuca, Inc.
3910 S. Yellowstone
Idaho Falls, ID 83402
(208) 522-0700
www.melaleuca.com

▼ Men's Choice
(see Procter & Gamble)

▼ Mentadent
(see Church & Dwight Co., Inc.)

DNR Mera-Naturals
P.O. Box 218
Circle Pines, MN 55014
(800) 752-7261; (763) 767-2224

DNR Merial Limited
3239 Satellite Blvd.
Duluth, GA 30096-4640
(888) 637-4251

DNR Merle Norman Cosmetics
9130 Bellanca Ave.
Los Angeles, CA 90045
(800) 421-2060; (310) 641-3000
www.merlenorman.com

◆ Meta Henna Créme
(see Dena Corp.)

DNR Mia Rose Products, Inc.
177 Riverside Ave., Ste. F
Newport Beach, CA 92663
(800) 292-6339; (714) 662-5465
www.miarose.com

❤ Michael Kors fragrances
(see Estee Lauder Companies)

❤ Millenium
(see Elizabeth Arden, Inc.)

▼ Miss Clairol
(see Procter & Gamble)

▼ Miss Kiss
(see Del Laboratories, Inc.)

❤ Mitchum
(see Revlon, Inc.)

◆ Mizani
(see L'Oreal)

DNR Model Secrets
(see Progressive Beauty Brands)

❤ Moiststic
(see TCCD Int'l, Inc.)

▼ Monistat
(see Personal Products Co.)

DNR Montagne Jeunesse
The Old Grain Store, 4 Denne Rd.
Horsham, West Sussex,
RH12 1JE, England
(800) 447-1919

❤ Moose products
(see Mad Gab's)

▼ Mop & Glo
(see Reckitt-Benckiser plc)

◆ Motherlove herbal co. ■
P.O. Box 101, 3101 Kintzley Plz.
Laporte, CO 80535-0101
(970) 493-2892
www.motherlove.com
Personal Care

❤ Mother's Special Blend
(see Mountain Ocean Ltd.)

❤ Motions
(see Alberto Culver)

❤ Mountain Ocean Ltd. ■
5150 Valmont Rd.
Boulder, CO 80301
(303) 444-2781
www.mountainocean.com
Personal Care

❤ Mountain Rose Herbs ■ ▣
P.O. Box 50220
Eugene, OR 97405-8656
(800) 879-3337
www.mountainroseherbs.com
*Companion Animal Care, Cosmetics,
Personal Care*

DNR Mr. Bubble
(see Playtex Products, Inc.)

▼ Mr. Clean
(see Procter & Gamble)

▼ Mr. Muscle
(see S.C. Johnson)

DNR Mudd
(see Chattem, Inc.)

DNR Murad, Inc.
2121 Rosecrans Ave., 5th Fl.
El Segundo, CA 90245
(888) 99-MURAD
www.murad.com

▼ Murphy Oil Soap
(see Colgate-Palmolive Co.)

DNR MW Laboratories
2002 52nd St. Extension
Savannah, GA 31405
(912) 236-9430
www.mwlabs.com

◆ My Skin
(see Dena Corp.)

❤ Mystic fragrance
(see Marilyn Miglin, L.P.)

▼ N.Y.C. New York Color
(see Del Laboratories, Inc.)

◆ NAACO ✳ ■
444 E. Gardena Blvd.
Gardena, CA 90248
(310) 352-6999
www.earthsafe.net
Household, Personal Care

DNR Nadina's Cremes
3813 Middletown Branch Rd.
Vienna, MD 21869-1533
(800) 722-4292; (410) 901-1052
www.nadinascremes.com

▼ Nair
(see Church & Dwight Co., Inc.)

DNR National Chemical Co.
4044 Lake Mary Blvd., Ste. 104
Lake Mary, FL 32746
(407) 425-9618
www.citruscleanit.com

DNR Native Scents, Inc.
1040 Dea Ln., Box # 5639
Taos, NM 87571
(800) 645-3471; (505) 758-9656
www.nativescents.com

❤ Natracare LLC ✳ ■
14901 E. Hampden, Ste. 190
Aurora, CO 80014
(303) 617-3476
www.natracare.com
Personal Care

DNR Natural Animal, Inc.
7000 US 1 N., P.O. Box 1177
St. Augustine, FL 32095
(800) 274-7387; (904) 824-5884
www.naturalanimal.com

▼ Natural Instincts
(see Procter & Gamble)

DNR Natural Products for Pets
2832 Ste. B Walnut Ave.
Tustin, CA 92780
(888) 644-7297

DNR Natural Research People Inc.
800 Dean Creek Rd.
Lavina, MT 59046
(406) 575-4343

DNR Natural Resource Group
1340-G Industrial Ave.
Petaluma, CA 94952
(888) 674-2344; (707)763-0662

DNR Natural Way Natural Body Care
822 Massachusetts St.
Lawrence, KS 66044
(785) 841-0100
www.naturalway.com

▼ Naturalamb Condoms
(see Church & Dwight Co., Inc.)

◆ Naturally Beautiful ⊡
P.O. Box 770
Kelseyville, CA 95451
(800) 440-7285
Personal Care

❤ Naturally Fresh Deodorant Crystal
(see TCCD Int'l, Inc.)

❤ Nature Clean products
(see Frank T. Ross & Sons, Ltd.)

DNR NaturElle Cosmetics Corp.
4777 Leyden
Denver, CO 80205
(800) 442-3936
www.naturalbeauty.com

DNR Nature's Gate
(see Levlad, Inc./Nature's Gate)

▼ Naturistics
(see Del Laboratories, Inc.)

▼ Nautica fragrances
(see Unilever)

▼ Neat Sheet
(see Kimberly-Clark Corp.)

DNR Nelson Bach USA Ltd.
100 Research Dr.
Wilmington, MA 01887
(800) 319-9151; (978) 988-3833
www.nelsonbach.com

DNR Neo Tech Cosmetic, Inc.
20626 Belshaw Ave.
Carson, CA 90746
(800) 432-3787; (310) 898-1640

DNR NeoStrata Co.
Four Research Way
Princeton, NJ 08540
(800) 865-8667; (609) 520-0715
www.neostrata.com

DNR Neoteric Cosmetics
4880 Havana St.
Denver, CO 80239
(800) 55-ALPHA; (303) 373-4860

❧ Neutrogena Corp. ■
5760 W. 96th St.
Los Angeles, CA 90045-5544
(800) 421-6857; (310) 642-1150
www.neutrogena.com
Personal Care
(see Johnson & Johnson)

DNR New Chapter, Inc.
22 High St.
Brattleboro, VT 05302
(800) 543-7279

DNR New Dana Perfumes
6601 Lyons Rd., Ste. B4
Coconut Creek, FL 33073
(877) 354-2239; (954) 725-6810

❤ New Methods ✳ ⌑
713 S. Main St., #C1
Willits, CA 95490
(707) 456-1262
Companion Animal Care

DNR Neways Generations
(see Neways Int'l)

DNR Neways Int'l
2089 W. Neways Dr.
Springville, VT 84663
(810) 418-2000
www.neways.com

DNR Newbrite
(see Neways Int'l)

❤ Nexxus Products Co. ■
P.O. Box 1274
82 Corner Dr.
Santa Barbara, CA 93116
(805) 968-6900
www.nexxusproducts.com
Personal Care

▼ Nice 'n Easy
(see Procter & Gamble)

◆ Nice N' Fluffy
(see USA Detergents)

▼ Nicoderm
(see GlaxoSmithKline Consumer
Healthcare)

▼ Nicorette
(see GlaxoSmithKline Consumer
Healthcare)

❤ Niora ✳■
24855 W. Brush Creek Rd.
Sweet Home, OR 97386-9614
(800) 882-9887; (541) 367-8629
www.niora.com
Personal Care

DNR NIOXIN Research Laboratories, Inc.
2124 Skyview Dr.
Lithia Springs, GA 30122
(800) 628-9890; (770) 944-1308
www.nioxin.com

◆ Nivea
(see Beiersdorf, Inc.)

▼ No More Tears
(see Johnson & Johnson)

▼ NO-AD products
(see Solar Cosmetic Labs, Inc.)

DNR Nomads Bath and Beauty Bazaar
207 Shelby St.
Santa Fe, NM 87501
(800) 360-4807; (505) 986-0855
www.nomads-santafe.com

❤ Norimoor Co., Inc. ✳■
3801 23rd Ave., Ste. 6
Astoria, NY 11105
(718) 721-6667
www.herbalmelange.com
Personal Care

DNR Northern Labs, Inc.
P.O. Box 850
Manitowoc, WI 54221
(920) 684-7137

❧ Norwegian Formula
(see Neutrogena Corp.)

DNR NOW Foods
395 S. Glen Ellyn Rd.
Bloomingdale, IL 60108
(888) 669-3663
www.naturesapothecary.com

DNR NOW® Products, Inc.
P.O. Box 27608
Tempe, AZ 85285-7608
(800) 662-0333
www.nowclean.com

▼ Noxema
(see Procter & Gamble)

DNR Nu Expressions
(see Bronner Brothers)

DNR Nu Skin Enterprises
75 W. Center St.; One Nu Skin Plaza
Provo, Utah 84601
(800) 877-6100; (801) 345-1000
www.nuskin.com

▼ Nuances
(see Procter & Gamble)

DNR Nutra Nail
(see CCA Industries, Inc.)

❤ Nutribiotic ■
P.O. Box 238
Lakeport, CA 95453
(800) 225-4345
www.nutribiotic.com
Personal Care

◆ Nutri-Cell, Inc. ✳ ■
1038 N. Tustin, Ste. 309
Orange, CA 92667-5958
(714) 953-8307
Personal Care

DNR Nutrimalt
(see St. JON Laboratories)

DNR Nutro Products, Inc.
445 Wilson Way
City of Industry, CA 91744
(800) 833-5330
www.nutroproducts.com

▼ o.b. Tampons
(see Personal Products Co.)

❤ Ocean Pacific fragrances
(see Parlux Fragrances, Inc.)

DNR Ocean Potion
(see Sun & Skin Care Research, Inc.)

▼ O'Cedar
(see Reckitt-Benckiser plc)

DNR O-Cel-O
(see 3M™)

DNR Odor Disposers
(see St. JON Laboratories)

◆ Odor-B-Gone products
(see Gannon's, Inc.)

▼ OFF! products
(see S.C. Johnson)

DNR Ogilvie
(see Playtex Products, Inc.)

DNR Ohio Hempery
7002 State Rte. 329
Guysville, OH 45735
(800) BUY-HEMP
www.hempery.com

▼ Ohm by Olay
(see Procter & Gamble)

◆ Oil-Dri Corp. of America ✳■
410 N. Michigan Ave., Ste. 400
Chicago, IL 60611
(800) 634-0315; (312) 321-1515
www.oildri.com
Companion Animal Care

▼ Olay
(see Procter & Gamble)

▼ Old English
(see Reckitt-Benckiser plc)

▼ Old Spice
(see Procter & Gamble)

◆ Ombrelle
(see L'Oreal)

◆ One Touch ■
2220 Gaspar Ave.
Los Angeles, CA 90040
(323) 728-2999
www.aiibeauty.com
Cosmetics, Personal Care
(see American Int'l Ind.)

DNR OPI Products, Inc.
13034 Saticoy St.
N. Hollywood, CA 91605
(800) 341-9999; (818) 759-2400
www.opi.com

◆ Optikem Int'l, Inc. ✳■
2172 S. Jason St.
Denver, CO 80223
(800) 525-1752; (303) 936-1137
Personal Care

DNR Optimal Plus
(see Neways Int'l)

▼ Orajel
(see Del Laboratories, Inc.)

▼ Oral-B
(see Gillette Co.)

DNR Orange Glo Int'l
8765 E. Richard Rd., Ste. 703
Englewood, CO 80111
(303) 740-1909
www.greatcleaners.com

❤ Orange-Mate Inc. ✳■
P.O. Box 883
Waldport, OR 97394
(800) 626-8685; (541) 563-3290
www.orangemate.com
Household

DNR Oregon Soap, Co.
P.O. Box 14464
Portland, OR 97293-0464
(800) 549-0299
www.oregonsoapco.com

◆ Organic Essentials ✳■
822 Baldridge St.
O'Donnell, TX 79351
(800) 765-6491; (806) 428-3486
www.organicessentials.com
Personal Care

DNR Organics
(see Levlad, Inc./Nature's Gate)

❤ Origins
(see Estee Lauder Companies)

DNR Orjene Natural Cosmetics Co., Inc.
543 48th Ave.
Long Island City, NY 11101-5694
(800) 886-7536; (718) 937-2666
www.orjenenaturalcosmetics.com

❤ Orlane, Inc. ✳■▱
555 Madison Ave., 11th Fl.
New York, NY 10022
(212) 750-1111
www.orlaneparis.com
Cosmetics, Personal Care
(see Perlier Kelemata)

◆ Orly Int'l, Inc. ✳ ■
9309 Deering Ave.
Chatsworth, CA 91311
(818) 998-1111
www.orlybeauty.com
Cosmetics

▼ Oust
(see S.C. Johnson)

▼ Oxy
(see GlaxoSmithKline
Consumer Healthcare)

▼ Oxyfresh Worldwide, Inc. ■
1875 N. Lakewood Dr.
Coeur d'Alene, ID 83814
(800) 333-7374
www.oxyfresh.com
*Companion Animal Care, Household,
Personal Care*

DNR Paco Rabanne Parfums
70 E. 55th St., 17th Fl.
New York, NY 10022
(212) 980-9620
www.pacorabanne.com

DNR Pacquin
(see Pfizer)

▼ Palmolive products
(see Colgate-Palmolive Co.)

◆ Paloma Picasso
(see L'Oreal)

▼ Pampers
(see Procter & Gamble)

▼ Pantene
(see Procter & Gamble)

DNR Para Laboratories, Inc.
100 Rose Ave.
Hempstead, NY 11550
(800) 645-3752; (516) 538-4600
www.queenhelene.com

◆ Parker & Bailey ✳ ■
35 Depot Rd.
Falmouth, ME 04105
(207) 781-5004
www.parkerbailey.com
Household

♥ Parlux Fragrances, Inc. ■
3725 S.W. 30th Ave.
Fort Lauderdale, FL 33312
(954) 316-9008
www.parlux.com
Cosmetics

▼ Parsons' Ammonia
(see Church & Dwight Co., Inc.)

◆ Patricia Allison ■ ▣
4470 Monahan Rd.
La Mesa, CA 91941
(800) 858-8742; (619) 444-4879
Cosmetics, Personal Care

DNR Patti Labelle fragrance
(see Color Me Beautiful, Inc.)

DNR Paul Mazzotta, Inc.
P.O. Box 96
Reading, PA 19607
(610) 376-2250

DNR Paul Mitchell products
(see John Paul Mitchell Systems)

♥ Paul Penders Co., Inc. ✳ ■
215 Center Ct.
San Pablo, CA 94806
(510) 691-3176
www.paulpenders.com
Cosmetics, Personal Care

◆ Paula's Choice ■ ▣
13075 Gateway Dr., Ste. 160
Seattle, WA 98118
(206) 444-1616
www.paulaschoice.com
Cosmetics, Personal Care

◆ P-Bee Products, Inc. ■
23011 Moulton Pkwy., Ste. F-7
Laguna Hills, CA 92653
(800) 322-5572; (949) 586-6300
www.pbeeproducts.com
Personal Care

DNR PCJ hair products
(see Luster Products, Inc.)

▼ Pearl Drops
(see Church & Dwight Co., Inc.)

◆ Peelu USA ☀ ■
4075 40th Ave. SW
Fargo, ND 58104
(701) 356-2812
Personal Care

◆ Penn Herb Co., Ltd. ■ ⋯
10601 Decatur Rd., Ste. 2
Philadelphia, PA 19154-3293
(215) 632-6100
www.pennherb.com
Personal Care

DNR Penny Island Products
P.O. Box 521
Graton, CA 95444-0521
(707) 823-2406

▼ Pepsodent
(see Church & Dwight Co., Inc.)

DNR Perlier Kelemata
555 Madison Ave.
New York, NY 10022
Cosmetics, Personal Care

❤ Perry Ellis fragrances
(see Parlux Fragrances, Inc.)

DNR Person & Covey
616 Allen Ave.
Glendale, CA 91201
(818) 240-1030
www.personandcovey.com

▼ Personal Products Co. ■
199 Grandview Rd.
Skillman, NJ 08558-9418
(908) 874-1000
www.itsmybody.com
Personal Care
(see Johnson & Johnson)

DNR Personna
(see American Safety Razor Co.)

▼ Pert Plus
(see Procter & Gamble)

DNR Pet Relief
(see St. JON Laboratories)

DNR Pet Tech, Inc.
P.O. Box 2285
Carlsbad, CA 92018
(760) 930-0309
www.pettech.net

DNR Petal Fresh Naturals
(see Levlad, Inc./Nature's Gate)

DNR PetGuard, Inc.
P.O. Box 668
Green Cove Springs, FL 32043
(800) 874-3221
www.petguard.com

DNR Petrodex
(see St. JON Laboratories)

DNR Petromalt
(see St. JON Laboratories)

DNR Pfizer
182 Tabor Rd.
Morris Plains, NJ 07950-2693
(800) 223-0182; (201)540-2000
www.pfizer.com

DNR Pharmagel Corp.
P.O. Box 2288
Monterey, CA 93942-2288
(800) 882-4889

DNR Phat Hair
(see Progressive Beauty Brands)

❤ Pheromone fragrance
(see Marilyn Miglin, L.P.)

DNR Philip B. Hair & Body Care
815 Alcott St.
Los Angeles, CA 90035
(800) 643-5556; (310) 659-3066

DNR Philosophy, Inc.
4602 E. Hammond Ln.
Phoenix, AZ 85034
(480) 736-8200
www.philosophy.com

DNR pHisoderm
(see Chattem, Inc.)

DNR Phybiosis
P.O. Box 6135, 5409 Bennett Ln.
Glen Allen, VA 23058-6135
(888) FOR-CLAY; (301) 805-7920
www.phybiosis.com

▼ Physique
(see Procter & Gamble)

◆ Pickering & Simmons ▨
777 New Durham Rd.
Edison, NJ 08817-2859
(800) 352-8777
www.norfolklavender.com
Household, Personal Care

DNR Pine Glo
(see Pine Glo Products, Inc.)

DNR Pine Glo Products, Inc.
P.O. Box 429, 404 S. Main St.
Rolesville, NC 27571
(919) 556-7787
www.pinegloproducts.com

▼ Pine-Sol
(see Clorox Co.)

DNR Pink hair products
(see Luster Products, Inc.)

DNR Placenta Plus
(see Progressive Beauty Brands)

❤ Planet Inc. ✳ ■
P.O. Box 48184, 3575 Douglas St.
Victoria, BC, Canada V8Z 7H6
(800) 858-8449; (250) 478-8171
www.planetinc.com
Household

DNR Plax
(see Pfizer)

DNR Playtex Products, Inc.
300 Nyala Farms Rd.
Westport, CT 06880
(203) 341-4000
www.playtexproductsinc.com

DNR Playtex Tampons
(see Playtex Products, Inc.)

▼ Pledge
(see S.C. Johnson)

◆ Plumbers Aid
(see USA Detergents)

DNR Plus+White
(see CCA Industries, Inc.)

▼ Poise
(see Kimberly-Clark Corp.)

▼ Polident
(see GlaxoSmithKline Consumer Healthcare)

▼ Poligrip
(see GlaxoSmithKline Consumer Healthcare)

▼ Ponds
(see Unilever)

▼ Porcelana
(see Schwarzkopf & Dep Inc.)

DNR Post-It
(see 3M™)

❤ Pout ✳■
28 Shelton St.
London WC2H 9JE
United Kingdom
www.pout.co.uk
Cosmetics

◆ Power Scrub
(see USA Detergents)

DNR Prairie Meadows Herbal Soap Co.
P.O. Box 292356
Phelan, CA 92329
(760) 868-4350

DNR Precious Aromatherapy
P.O. Box 17155
Boulder, CO 80308
(800) 877-6889; (303) 447-1667
www.aromatherapy.com

❧ Prescription Diet
(see Hill's Pet Nutrition)

❤ Prescriptives
(see Estee Lauder Companies)

DNR Prestige Cosmetics
1441 W. Newport Center Dr.
Deerfield Beach, FL 33442
(954) 480-9202
www.prestigecosmetics.net

DNR Pretty Baby Herbal Soap
P.O. Box 555
China Grove, NC 28023
(800) 673-8167
www.prettybabysoap.com

♥ Prima Fleur Botanicals, Inc. ✳ ■
1525 E. Francisco Blvd., Ste. 16
San Rafael, CA 94901
(415) 455-0957
www.primafleur.com
Personal Care

DNR Principal Secret
41550 Eclectic St., Ste. 200
Palm Desert, CA 92260
(800) 545-5595
www.principal-secret.com

▼ Procter & Gamble ■
P.O. Box 599
Cincinnati, OH 45201
(800) 331-3774; (513) 983-1100
www.pg.com
*Companion Animal Care, Household,
Personal Care*

DNR Procyte Corp.
P.O. Box 808
Redmond, WA 98073
(888) 966-1010; (425) 869-1239
www.procyte.com

DNR Professional Pet Products
1873 NW 97th Ave.
Miami, FL 33172
(800) 432-5349; (305) 592-1992

DNR Progressive Beauty Brands
2700 E. 28Th St.
Minneapolis, MN 55406-1510
(800) 326-7256; (612) 546-0322
www.progressivebeautybrands.com

DNR Pro-Line Corp.
P.O. Box 223706
Dallas, TX 75222
(800) 527-5879; (214) 631-4247
www.prolinecorp.com

▼ Pronto
(see Del Laboratories, Inc.)

DNR Pro-Tec Pet Health
5440 Camus Rd.
Carson City, NV 89701-9306
(800) 44-FLEAS; (775) 884-2566
www.protec-pet-health.com

♥ PS Fine Cologne for Men
(see Elizabeth Arden, Inc.)

▼ Puffs
(see Procter & Gamble)

▼ Pull-Ups
(see Kimberly-Clark Corp.)

▼ PUR
(see Procter & Gamble)

DNR Pura-A-Teas
(see Progressive Beauty Brands)

▼ Pure & Natural
(see Dial Corp., Inc.)

♥ Pure Touch Therapeutics ✳ ■ ⊡
P.O. Box 234
Glen Ellen, CA 95442-0234
(800) 442-PURE; (707) 996-7817
www.puretouch.net
Personal Care

▼ Purex products
(see Dial Corp., Inc.)

▼ Q-Tips
(see Unilever)

DNR Queen Helene
(see Para Laboratories, Inc.)

▼ Quilted Northern
(see Georgia-Pacific)

◆ Rachel Perry, Inc. ■
15140 Keswick St.
Van Nuys, CA 91405
(800) 966-8888
www.rachelperry.net
Cosmetics, Personal Care

▼ Raid
(see S.C. Johnson)

▼ Rain Drops Water Softener
(see Church & Dwight Co., Inc.)

⦙ Rainbath
(see Neutrogena Corp.)

◆ Rainbow Research Corp. ■ ⊡
170 Wilbur Pl.
Bohemia, NY 11716
(800) 722-9595; (631) 589-5563
www.rainbowresearch.com
Personal Care

◆ Ralph Lauren
(see L'Oreal)

DNR Ranir Corp.
4701 E. Paris Ave. SE
Grand Rapids, MI 49512
(616) 698-8880

◆ Ravenwood ■
5110 M-72 West
Traverse City, MI 49684
(231) 929-4181
www.ravenwoodspa.com
Personal Care

▼ Reach
(see Personal Products Co.)

◆ Real Aloe Co. ■
P.O. Box 2770 1620 Fiske Pl.
Oxnard, CA 93033
(800) 541-7809
Personal Care

◆ Really Works
(see Vin-Dotco, Inc.)

▼ Reckitt-Benckiser plc ■
103-105 Bath Rd.
Slough, SL1 3UH Berks United
Kingdom
(44) 1753 217 800
www.reckittbenckiser.com
Household, Personal Care

❤ Red Door Revealed
(see Elizabeth Arden, Inc.)

◆ Redken
(see L'Oreal)

DNR Redmond Minerals, Inc.
6005 N. 100 West P.O. Box 219
Redmond, UT 84652
(800) 367-7258; (435) 529-7486
www.realsalt.com

DNR Refresh All Purpose Cleaner
(see Pine Glo Products, Inc.)

DNR Rembrandt Toothpaste &
Mouthwash
(see Den-Mat Corp.)

DNR Renew Carpet Cleaner
(see Pine Glo Products, Inc.)

▼ ReNu Solution
(see Bausch & Lomb Inc.)

▼ Renuzit products
(see Dial Corp., Inc.)

▼ Resolve
(see Reckitt-Benckiser plc)

DNR Reviva Labs, Inc.
705 Hopkins Rd.
Haddonfield, NJ 08033
(800) 257-7774; (609) 428-3885
www.revivalabs.com

❤ Revlon, Inc. ■
237 Park Ave.
New York, NY 10017
(800) 4-Revlon; (212) 527-4000
www.revlon.com
Cosmetics, Personal Care

▼ Right Guard
(see Gillette Co.)

DNR Rio Vista Products
520 S. Farnel Rd.
Santa Maria, CA 93458
(800) 248-6428
www.riovistaproducts.com

◆ RoC S.A. ■
199 Grandview Rd.
Skillman, NJ 08558-9418
(800) 762-1964
www.roc.com
Personal Care
(see Johnson & Johnson)

❤ Rodan+Fields
(see Estee Lauder Companies)

DNR Roebic Laboratories, Inc.
25 Connair Rd., P.O. Box 927
Orange, CT 06477
(203) 795-1283

DNR Royal Jelly
(see Jafra Cosmetics Int'l)

DNR Rusk Inc.
1 Cummings Point Rd.
Stamford, CT 06904
(800) Use-Rusk
www.rusk1.com

▼ S.C. Johnson ■
1525 Howe St.
Racine, WI 53403-2236
(800) 494-4855; (262) 260-2000
www.scjohnson.com
Household

▼ S.O.S.
(see Clorox Co.)

DNR Safe Choice
(see American Formulating & Mfg.)

DNR Safe Solutions, Inc.
1007 N. Cactus Trail
Seymour, TX 76380
(877) 554-5222
www.cactusjuicetm.com

▼ Safeguard
(see Procter & Gamble)

▼ Sally Hansen
(see Del Laboratories, Inc.)

▼ Salon Selectives
(see Unilever)

DNR Sanex
(see Sara Lee Corp.)

◆ Sappo Hill Soapworks ✳ ■
654 Tolman Creek Rd.
Ashland, OR 97520
(800) 863-7627; (541) 482-4485
www.sappohill.com
Personal Care

DNR Sara Lee Corp.
Three First National Plz.
Chicago, IL 60602-4260
(312) 726-2600
www.saralee.com

▼ Saran
(see S.C. Johnson)

▼ Satin Care
(see Gillette Co.)

DNR Scar Zone
(see CCA Industries, Inc.)

▼ Schering-Plough Corp. ■
2000 Galloping Hill Rd.
Kenilworth, NJ 07033-0530
(800) 822-7000; (908) 298-4000
www.sch-plough.com
Cosmetics, Personal Care

DNR Schroeder & Tremayne, Inc.
8450 Valcour
St. Louis, MO 63123
(800) 477-6643; (314) 349-5655

▼ Schwarzkopf & Dep Inc. ■
2101 E. Via Arado
Rancho Dominguez, CA 90220-6189
(310) 604-0777
www.dep.com
Cosmetics, Personal Care
(see Henkel KGaA)

🐾 Science Diet
(see Hill's Pet Nutrition)

▼ Scoop Away
(see Clorox Co.)

▼ Scope
(see Procter & Gamble)

DNR Scotch products
(see 3M™)

DNR Scotch-Brite
(see 3M™)

DNR Scotchgard
(see 3M™)

▼ Scott
(see Kimberly-Clark Corp.)

DNR Scotties
(see Irving Tissue, Inc.)

▼ Scrub Free
(see Church & Dwight Co., Inc.)

▼ Scrubbing Bubbles
(see S.C. Johnson)

◆ Scruples Professional Salon
Products, Inc. ✳ ■
8231-214th St., West
Lakeville, MN 55044-9102
(612) 469-4646
www.scrupleshaircare.com
Personal Care

DNR S-Curl hair products
(see Luster Products, Inc.)

🐾 Sebastian Int'l, Inc. ■
6109 DeSoto Ave.
Woodland Hills, CA 91367
(800) 829-7322; (818) 999-5112
www.sebastian-intl.com
Cosmetics, Personal Care
(see Wella Corp.)

▼ Secret
(see Procter & Gamble)

◆ Secret Gardens ✳ ■ ▣
P.O. Box 449 12199 Brem Ln.
Nevada City, CA 95959
(800) 537-8766; (530) 292-4330
Cosmetics, Personal Care

DNR Selsun Blue
(see Chattem, Inc.)

DNR Semodex
(see NIOXIN Research
Laboratories, Inc.)

DNR Senna Cosmetics
28042 Ave. Stanford
Valencia, CA 91355
(661) 257-3662
www.sennacosmetics.com

▼ Sensitive Eyes Solution
(see Bausch & Lomb Inc.)

▼ Sensodyne
(see GlaxoSmithKline
Consumer Healthcare)

▼ Sensor shaving products
(see Gillette Co.)

DNR Sergeant's Pet Care Products
1 Con Agra Dr.
Omaha, NE 68102
(402) 595-7000
www.sergeants.com

DNR SerVaas Laboratories Inc.
1200 Waterway Blvd.
Indianapolis, IN 46207
(800) 433-5818; (317) 636-7760

DNR Set-N-Me-Free Aloe Vera Co.
19220 SE Stark
Portland, OR 97233-5751
(800) 221-9727; (503) 666-9661

♥ Seventh Generation ✳ ■ ▣
212 Battery St., Ste. A
Burlington, VT 05401-5232
(802) 658-3773
www.seventhgeneration.com
Household, Personal Care

◆ Shadow Lake products
(see Citra-Solv, LLC)

❤ Shaklee Corp. ■
4747 Willow Rd.
Pleasanton, CA 94588
(800) SHAKLEE; (925) 924-2000
www.shaklee.com
Cosmetics, Household, Personal Care

◆ Sheer Blonde
(see Kao Brands Co. (formerly
Andrew Jergens Co.))

▼ Shield
(see Unilever)

❤ ShiKai Products ❋ ■
P.O. Box 2866
Santa Rosa, CA 95405
(800) 448-0298
www.shikai.com
Personal Care

◆ Shiseido Company Ltd. ■
900 Third Ave., 15th Fl.
New York, NY 10022
(212) 805-2300
www.shiseido.com
Cosmetics, Personal Care

▼ Shout
(see S.C. Johnson)

◆ Shu Uemura
(see L'Oreal)

▼ Signal Mouthwash
(see Unilever)

DNR Silver Brights
(see Advanced Research Laboratories)

❤ Simmons Natural Bodycare ■ ▣
42295 Hwy. 36
Bridgeville, CA 95526-9603
(707) 777-1920
www.simmonsnaturals.com
Personal Care

DNR Simple Green
(see Sunshine Makers, Inc.)

DNR Simpler Thyme®
P.O. Box 2858
Branchville, NJ 07826
(973) 875-9070

◆ Simplers Botanical Co. ❋ ■ ▣
P.O. Box 2534
Sebastol, CA 95476
(800) 652-7646; (707) 887-2012
www.simplers.com
Personal Care

DNR Simply Soap
6593 Delfern St.
San Diego, CA 92120
(619) 287-1394
www.simplysoap.com

▼ Skin Barrier
(see Oxyfresh Worldwide, Inc.)

▼ Skin Bracer
(see Colgate-Palmolive Co.)

DNR Skin Ceuticals Inc.
3402 Miller Rd.
Garland, TX 75041
(800) 811-1660; (972) 926-2900
www.skinceuticals.com

♥ skinsimple
(see Elizabeth Arden, Inc.)

▼ Skintastic
(see S.C. Johnson)

▼ Skintimate
(see S.C. Johnson)

♥ Smith & Vandiver, Inc. ■
480 Airport Blvd.
Watsonville, CA 95076
(831) 722-9526
www.smith-vandiver.com
Cosmetics, Personal Care

DNR Smooth 'N Shine
(see Advanced Research Laboratories)

DNR SNAP All Purpose Cleaner
(see Pine Glo Products, Inc.)

▼ Snobol
(see Church & Dwight Co., Inc.)

▼ Snuggle
(see Unilever)

DNR Soap Factory
188 Bunting Rd.
St. Catherines, Ontario, L2M 3Y1,
Canada
(905) 682-1808

▼ So-Dri
(see Georgia-Pacific)

♥ Soft & Beautiful
(see Alberto Culver)

▼ Soft & Dri
(see Gillette Co.)

▼ Soft 'n Gentle
(see Georgia-Pacific)

▼ Soft Scrub
(see Clorox Co.)

◆ Softsheen-Carson
(see L'Oreal)

▼ Softsoap products
(see Colgate-Palmolive Co.)

DNR Softwave
(see Irving Tissue, Inc.)

DNR Sojourner Farms
1 19th Ave. S
Minneapolis, MN 55454-1021
(888) 867-6567
www.sojos.com

▼ Solar Cosmetic Labs, Inc. ✳ ■
4920 NW 165th St.
Miami, FL 33014
(800) 327-3991; (305) 621-5551
www.no-ad.com
Personal Care

DNR Solar Sense
(see CCA Industries, Inc.)

▼ Solarcaine
(see Schering-Plough Corp.)

DNR Solid Gold Health Products
for Pets, Inc.
900 Vernon Way, #101
El Cajon, CA 92020
(800) 364- 4863; (619) 258-2780
www.solidgoldhealth.com

DNR Sombra Cosmetics Inc.
5951 Office Blvd. NE
Albuquerque, NM 87109-5822
(800) 225-3963; (505) 888-0288
www.sorenomoreusa.com

♥ Sonoma Soap Co.
(see Avalon Natural Products)

DNR Sothy's USA
1500 N.W. 94th Ave.
Miami, FL 33172
(800) 325-0503

▼ Sparkle
(see Georgia-Pacific)

DNR Sparkle Glass Cleaner
(see A.J. Funk & Co.)

DNR Specialty Products, Inc.
10300 Farm Rd. 1902
Crowley, TX 76036
(800) 860-1615

▼ Speed Stick
(see Colgate-Palmolive Co.)

▼ Spray 'n Wash
(see Reckitt-Benckiser plc)

❤ St. Ives Laboratories ■
2525 Armitage Ave.
Melrose Park, IL 60160-1163
(708) 450-3000
www.stives.com
Personal Care
(see Alberto-Culver)

❤ St. John's Herb Garden, Inc. ■ ▣
7711 Hillmeade Rd.
Bowie, MD 20720
(301) 262-5302
www.st-johns.com
Cosmetics, Personal Care

DNR St. JON Laboratories
1656 W. 240th St.
Harbor City, CA 90710
(800) 969-7387
www.mardel-labs.com/stjon

▼ StaFlo starch
(see Dial Corp., Inc.)

DNR Star Brite
4041 S.W. 47th Ave.
Fort Lauderdale, FL 33314
(800) 327-8583; (305) 587-6280

DNR Star Burst glitter gels
(see Progressive Beauty Brands)

◆ Starwest Botanicals, Inc. ■
11253 Trade Center Dr.
Rancho Cordova, CA 95742
(800) 800-4372; (916) 853-9354
www.starwest-botanicals.com
Personal Care

❤ Static Guard
(see Alberto Culver)

▼ Stayfree
(see Personal Products Co.)

DNR Stevens Research Salon Products
19417 63rd Ave. NE
Arlington, WA 98223
(800) 262-3344; (360) 435-4513
www.stevensresearch.com

❤ Stick-With-Us Products, Inc. ✳ ■
P.O. Box 331
Pt. Roberts, WA 98281
(604) 241-0448
www.moom.com
Cosmetics, Personal Care

❤ Stila
(see Estee Lauder Companies)

DNR Strong Skin Savvy, Inc.
1 Lakeside Dr.
New Providence, PA 17560
(800) 724-3952; (717) 786-8947
www.strongskinsavvy.com

DNR Studio Magic, Inc.
20135-Cypress Creek Dr.
Alva, FL 33920-3305
(800) 452-7706; (239) 728-3344
www.studiomagic.cc

▼ Suave
(see Unilever)

▼ Suavitel
(see Colgate-Palmolive Co.)

DNR Sudden Change
(see CCA Industries, Inc.)

DNR Sue's Amazing Lip Stuff
P.O. Box 64
Westby, WI 54667
(877) 786-3649; (608) 634-2988
www.sundoghemp.com

DNR Sun & Earth, Inc.
125 Noble St.
Norristown, PA 19401
(800) 298-7861
www.sunandearth.com

DNR Sun & Skin Care Research, Inc.
851 Greensboro Rd.
Cocoa, FL 32926
(800) 715-3485
www.opotion.com

DNR Sun Dog products
(see Sue's Amazing Lip Stuff)

♥ Sunfeather Natural Soap Co. ■ ▣
1551 Hwy. 72
Potsdam, NY 13676
(315) 265-3648
www.sunsoap.com
Companion Animal Care,
Personal Care

♥ Sunflowers fragrance
(see Elizabeth Arden, Inc.)

DNR Sun-in
(see Chattem, Inc.)

▼ Sunlight
(see Unilever)

DNR Sunpoint products, inc.
P.O. Box 567
Lawrence, MA 01842
(978) 794-3100
www.sunpointinc.com

◆ Sunrise Lane ▣
780 Greenwich St.
New York, NY 10014
(212) 242-7014
Companion Animal Care, Household,
Personal Care

DNR Sunshine Makers, Inc.
15922 Pacific Coast Hwy.
Huntington Harbour, CA 92649
(800) 228-0709; (562) 795-6000
www.simplegreen.com

DNR Sunshine Oils
2545 Prairie Rd.
Eugene, OR 97402
(800) 659-2077

DNR Sunstar Butler
4635 W. Foster Ave.
Chicago, IL 60630
(888) 777-3101; (773) 777-4000
www.jbutler.com

◆ Supernail Professional ■
2220 Gaspar Ave.
Los Angeles, CA 90040
(323) 728-2999
www.aiibeauty.com
Cosmetics, Personal Care
(see American Int'l Ind.)

DNR Surco Products, Inc.
RIDC Industrial Park, 292 Alpha Dr.
Pittsburgh, PA 15238-2903
(800) 556-0111; (412) 252-7000

▼ Sure
(see Procter & Gamble)

▼ Surf
(see Unilever)

DNR Susan Lucci Enterprises
107 7th St.
Garden City, NY 11530
(877) 525-8224
www.susanlucci.com

▼ Swiffer
(see Procter & Gamble)

❤ Swiss Formula products
(see St. Ives Laboratories)

◆ Swiss Pine
(see USA Detergents)

◆ T.N. Dickinson's Witch Hazel
(see Dickinson Brands Inc.)

❧ T/Gel
(see Neutrogena Corp.)

▼ Tampax
(see Procter & Gamble)

DNR Tanning Research Labs, Inc.
P.O. Box 265111
Daytona Beach, FL 32126
(386) 677-9559
www.hawaiiantropic.com

DNR Tarn-X
(see Jelmar, Inc.)

❤ TARRAH Cosmetics ▣
P.O. Box 243209
Boynton Beach, FL 33424-3209
(561) 374-5995
www.tarrah.com
Cosmetics, Personal Care

DNR TaUT Skin Care and Cosmetics
P.O. Box 1870
Simi Valley, CA 93062
(800) 438-8288; (805) 522-8390
www.tautcosmetics.com

❤ TCB hair products
(see Alberto Culver)

TCCD Int'l, Inc. ✳■▣
2301 NW 33rd Ct., Ste. 103
Pompano Beach, FL 33069-1000
(800) 653-4006; (954) 960-4904
www.tccd.com
Personal Care

▼ Teen Spirit
(see Colgate-Palmolive Co.)

DNR Tender Corp.
P.O. Box 290
Littleton, NH 03561-3957
(800) 258-4696; (603) 444-5464
www.tendercorp.com

❤ Terrapin
(see Earth Essentials)

❤ TerrEssentials ■▣
2650 Old National Pike
Middletown, MD 21769-8817
(301) 371-7333
www.terressentials.com
Personal Care

◆ Terry Binns SkinCare, Inc. ▣
8201 Mission Rd., #200
Prairie Village, KS 66208
(800) 909-7546; (913) 722-6522
www.terrybinns.com
Cosmetics, Personal Care

◆ Texas Best UnLimited, LP ■
P.O. Box 290769 3401
Fredericksburg
Kerrville, TX 78029-0769
(830) 257-6020
Personal Care

❤ The Body Shop ■
5036 One World Way
Wake Forest, NC 27587
(919) 554-4900
www.bodyshop.com
Cosmetics, Household, Personal Care

DNR The Bramton Co.
P.O. Box 655450
Dallas, TX 75265-5450
(800) 272-6336
www.bramton.com

▼ The Iams Company ■
7250 Poe Ave.
Dayton, OH 45414-2547
(800) 675-3849; (937) 898-7387
www.iams.com
Companion Animal Care
(see Procter & Gamble)

◆ the organic way
(see Dena Corp.)

DNR The Terrapin Companies
P.O. Box 40339
Santa Barbara, CA 93140-0339
(800) 347-5211
www.goturtle.com

▼ Thermacare
(see Procter & Gamble)

▼ ThermaSilk
(see Unilever)

DNR Thibiant Int'l Inc.
449 N. Canon Dr.
Beverly Hills, CA 90210
(800) 825-2517; (310) 659-1970
www.thibiantspa.com

DNR Thicker Fuller Hair
(see Advanced Research Laboratories)

DNR Thinsulate
(see 3M™)

▼ Tide
(see Procter & Gamble)

DNR Tiffany & Co.
727 Fifth Ave.
New York, NY 10022
(212) 755-8000
www.tiffany.com

◆ Tile Action
(see USA Detergents)

▼ Tilex
(see Clorox Co.)

▼ Tinactin
(see Schering-Plough Corp.)

DNR Tisserand Aromatherapy
Newtown Road, Hove
Sussex , BN3 7BA England
44 (0)1273 325666
www.tisserand.com

- ▼ Toilet Duck
  (see S.C. Johnson)

- ❤ Tommy Hilfiger products
  (see Estee Lauder Companies)

- ❤ Tom's of Maine, Inc. ■
  P.O. Box 710
  Kennebunk, ME 04043-0710
  (800) 367-8667; (207) 985-2944
  www.tomsofmaine.com
  Personal Care

- ▼ Tone
  (see Dial Corp., Inc.)

- ▼ Topol toothpaste
  (see Schwarzkopf & Dep Inc.)

- ❤ Totally Juicy
  (see Freeman Beauty)

- ❤ Totally Nutty
  (see Freeman Beauty)

- ◆ Touch of Glass
  (see USA Detergents)

- ▼ Trac II
  (see Gillette Co.)

- ▼ Trend detergent
  (see Dial Corp., Inc.)

- ❤ TRESemme
  (see Alberto Culver)

- ▼ Trojan Condoms
  (see Church & Dwight Co., Inc.)

- DNR Tropez cosmetics
  (see Markwins International Corp.
  (formerly AM Cosmetics))

- DNR Trophy Animal Health Care
  8809 Ely St.
  Pensacola, FL 32514-7064
  (800) 336-7087
  www.trophyanimalcare.com

- DNR Tropical Botanicals
  P.O. Box 635
  Ramona, CA 92065
  (760) 788-4480

- DNR Tropix Suncare Products
  1014 Laurel St.
  Brainerd, MN 56401
  (800) 421-7314

DNR Tucks
(see Pfizer)

▼ Tuffy
(see Clorox Co.)

DNR Twincraft Soap Co.
2 Tigan St.
Winooski, VT 05404
(800) 792-7377; (802) 655-2200

DNR Udder Wize
(see Progressive Beauty Brands)

❤ Ultima II
(see Revlon, Inc.)

◆ Ultra Shine
(see Dena Corp.)

DNR Ultra Swim
(see Chattem, Inc.)

▼ Ultress
(see Procter & Gamble)

DNR Unelko Corp.
14641 N. 74th St.
Scottsdale, AZ 85260
(408) 991-7272
www.unelko.com

▼ Unilever ■
920 Sylvan Ave., 2nd Fl.
Englewood Cliffs, NJ 07632
(866) 204-9750
www.unileverna.com
Cosmetics, Personal Care
(see Unilever Plc)

▼ Unilever Plc ■
Unilever House P.O. Box 68
Blackfriars London, EC4P 4BQ
United Kingdom
(44) 20 7822 5252
www.unilever.com
Cosmetics, Household, Personal Care

❤ Universal Light ✳ ■
1100 Lotus Dr.
Silver Lake, WI 53170
(262) 889-8571
Personal Care

❤ Un-petroleum
(see Avalon Natural Products)

❤ Urban Decay ■
729 Farad St.
Costa Mesa, CA 92627
(800) 784-8722; (949) 515-1250
www.urbandecay.com
Cosmetics
(see Hard Candy)

◆ USA Detergents ✳ ■
1735 Jersey Ave., Ste. 2
North Brunswick, NJ 08902
(732) 828-1800
www.usa-detergents.com
Household

DNR USA Labs, Inc.
8055 NW 77 Ct., Ste. 5
Miami, FL 33166
(800) 831-6341; (305) 888-8025
www.usalabsinc.com

▼ Valentino fragrances
(see Unilever)

◆ Vanda Beauty Counselors, Inc. ▣
P.O. Box 3433
Orlando, FL 32803
(407) 839-0223
www.vandabeautycounselor.com
Cosmetics, Personal Care

▼ Vanish
(see S.C. Johnson)

▼ Vanity Fair
(see Georgia-Pacific)

▼ Vaseline
(see Unilever)

▼ Veet
(see Reckitt-Benckiser plc)

❤ VeganEssentials ✳ ▣
3707 N. 92nd St.
Milwaukee, WI 53222
(866) 88-VEGAN; (414) 527-9684
www.veganessentials.com
*Companion Animal Care, Cosmetics,
Household, Personal Care*

▼ Venus shaving products
(see Gillette Co.)

▼ Vera Wang fragrances
(see Unilever)

❤ Vermont Soapworks ■ ▣
616 Exchange St.
Middlebury, VT 05753-1105
(802) 388-4302
www.vermontsoap.com
Companion Animal Care, Household, Personal Care

DNR Veterinarian's Best Inc.
P.O. Box 4459
Santa Barbara, CA 93140-4459
(800) 866-7387; (805) 963-9622
www.vetsbest.com

◆ Vichy Laboratories
(see L'Oreal)

DNR Victoria Jackson Cosmetics, Inc.
1230 American Blvd.
Westchester, PA 19380
(800) 848-7990
www.vjcosmetics.com

DNR Victoria's Secret
P.O. Box 16586
Columbus, OH 43216
(800) 411-5116
www.VictoriasSecret.com
(see Limited, Inc.)

▼ Vidal Sassoon
(see Procter & Gamble)

DNR ViJon Laboratories, Inc.
851 S. Page Ave.
St. Louis, MO 63114
(800) 325-8167
www.vijon.com

◆ Vin-Dotco, Inc. ■
2875 MCI Dr.
Pinellas Park, FL 33782
(800) 237-5911 ; (727) 217-9200
www.vindotco.com
Cosmetics, Household, Personal Care

❤ Visible Difference
(see Elizabeth Arden, Inc.)

DNR Visine
(see Pfizer)

DNR Vitabath
(see Esscentual Brands, LLC)

DNR Vitacost.com Inc.
2055 High Ridge Rd.
Boynton Beach, FL 33126
(800) 793-2601
www.vitacost.com

▼ Viva
(see Kimberly-Clark Corp.)

❤ VO5 products
(see Alberto Culver)

❤ V'tae Parfume & Body Care ■
569 Searls Ave.
Nevada City, CA 95959-3029
(800) 643-3011
www.vtae.com
Companion Animal Care,
Personal Care

◆ Wachters' Organic Sea
Products Corp. ✳ ■
550 Sylvan St.
Daly City, CA 94014
(800) 682-7100; (650) 757-9851
www.wachters.com
Companion Animal Care, Household,
Personal Care

◆ Warm Earth Cosmetics ■ ▫
1155 Stanley Ave.
Chico, CA 95928-6944
(530) 895-0455
www.geocities.com/warmearthcos-
metics
Cosmetics, Personal Care

DNR Warren Laboratories, Inc.
1656 IH 35 S
Abbott, TX 76621
(254) 580-9990
www.warrenlabsaloe.com

DNR Wash 'N Curl
(see CCA Industries, Inc.)

DNR Watkins Inc.
150 Liberty St., P.O. Box 5570
Winona, MN 55987
(800) 243-9423; (507) 457-3300
www.watkinsonline.com

◆ Wee
(see Indigo Wild Aromatics)

DNR Weleda, Inc.
175 N. Route, 9W
Congers, NY 10920
(845) 268-8572
www.weleda.com

❧ Wella Corp. ■
6109 DeSoto Ave.
Woodland Hills, CA 91367
(800) 456-9322
www.wellausa.com
Personal Care
(see Procter & Gamble)

DNR Wet 'N' Wild cosmetics
(see Markwins International Corp.
(formerly AM Cosmetics))

DNR Wet Ones
(see Playtex Products, Inc.)

DNR Whip-It Products, Inc.
P.O. Box 30128
Pensacola, FL 32503
(904) 436-2125
www.whip-it.net

❤ White Shoulders
(see Elizabeth Arden, Inc.)

▼ Windex
(see S.C. Johnson)

❤ Windrose Trading Co. ✳ ▣
P.O. Box 990, 108 Schoolhouse Rd.
Madison, VA 22727
(800) 229-3731; (540) 948-2268
www.windrosetrading.com
Personal Care

❤ Wings fragrance
(see Elizabeth Arden, Inc.)

❤ Wisdom Oral Care, Ltd. (formerly
CP2 Distribution, LLC) ■
444 Skokie Rd., Ste. 301
Wilmette, IL 60091
(866) 854-2650; (847) 256-3990
www.wisdomusa.com
Personal Care

❤ WiseWays Herbals ■
Singing Brook Farm, 99 Harvey Rd.
Worthington, MA 01098
(888)-540-1600; (413) 238-4268
www.wiseways.com
*Companion Animal Care, Cosmetics,
Household, Personal Care*

▼ Wisk
(see Unilever)

♥ Woodstock Natural Products, Inc. ✳ ■
140 Sylvan Ave.
Englewood Cliffs, NJ 07632
(800) 615-6895
www.thenaturaldentist.com
Personal Care

DNR Woolite carpet & laundry cleaners
(see Playtex Products, Inc.)

▼ Woolite fine fabric wash
(see Reckitt-Benckiser plc)

DNR World's Best Cat Litter
1600 Oregon St.
Muscatine, IA 52761-1494
(877) 367-9225

DNR Worldwide Cosmetics
12222 Sherman Way
North Hollywood, CA 91605
(800) 624-5776
www.worldwidecosmetics.com

♥ Wow-Bow Distributors, Ltd. ✳ ■ ⋯
13 B Lucon Dr.
Deer Park, NY 11729
(800) 326-0230; (631) 254-6064
www.wow-bow.com
Companion Animal Care

DNR Wysong Corp.
1880 N. Eastman Rd.
Midland, MI 48642-7779
(800) 748-0188; (989)631-0009
www.wysong.net

❧ Xtah
(see Sebastian Int'l, Inc.)

◆ Xtra detergent
(see USA Detergents)

◆ Y.U.M.
(see Indigo Wild Aromatics)

DNR Yardley of London
4135 Willow Lake Blvd., Bldg. #9
Memphis, TN 38118
(901) 547-7435
www.yardleylondon.com

DNR Yves Rocher North America Inc.
102 Pickering Way, Ste. 300
Exton, PA 19341-1330
(800) 321-YVES
www.yrbeauty.com

DNR Yves Saint Laurent Beaute, Inc.
90 Park Ave.
New York, NY 10016
(212) 551-4700

◆ ZAR
(see Indigo Wild Aromatics)

▼ Zee
(see Georgia-Pacific)

DNR Zelda's
154 Esopus Ave.
Kingston, NY 12401
(800) 647-8202

DNR Zema shampoo
(see St. JON Laboratories)

DNR Zenith Is 4 The Planet
P.O. Box 1739
Corvallis, OR 97339
(800) 547-2741
www.zenith4theplanet.com

DNR Zero Frizz
(see Advanced Research Laboratories)

▼ Zest
(see Procter & Gamble)

❤ Zhen, Inc. ■ ▣
2665 4th Ave. # 102A
Anoka, MN 55303
(800) 457-8455; (763) 323-4817
www.zhenbeauty.com
Cosmetics, Personal Care

❤ Zia Natural Skincare ■ ▣
1337 Evans Ave.
San Francisco, CA 94124
(800) 334-7546; (415) 642-8339
www.zianatural.com
Cosmetics, Personal Care

DNR Zip products
(see Lee Pharmaceuticals)

▼ Ziploc products
(see S.C. Johnson)

◆ Zip's
(see Indigo Wild Aromatics)

DNR ZNO Inc.
2425 S. Eastern Ave.
Commerce, CA 90040
(866) 604-0200; (323) 887-0200
www.ferity.com

DNR Zodiac Pet Products
1100 E. Woodfield Rd., Ste. 500
Schaumburg, IL 60173
(800) 950-4783
www.morethanapet.com

◆ Zotos Int'l, Inc. ■
100 Tokeneke Rd.
Darien, CT 06820-1005
(800) 242-9283; (203) 655-8911
www.zotos.com
Personal Care
(see Shiseido Cosmetics America)

▼ Zout
(see Dial Corp., Inc.)

◆ Zum
(see Indigo Wild Aromatics)

❤ ZuZu Luxe Cosmetics
(see Gabriel Cosmetics, Inc.)

Pursuin

Parent Companies Behind Product Names   138

Cruelty-Free Mail Order Companies   148

Animal-Derived Ingredients Used in Consumer Products   154

Health-Based Charities That DO and DO NOT
Fund Animal Research   156

Frequently Asked Questions and Answers About Animal Testing   184

he Cruelty-Free Way of Living

PARENT COMPANIES BEHIND PRODUCT NAMES

Following is a list of major companies and the brand names/products they manufacture. This list will help you identify the parent company of those brand names or products that may not be readily identifiable with its subsidiaries or divisions. For example, when you look under Colgate-Palmolive Co., you will see that one of its subsidiaries is Hill's Pet Nutrition, which manufactures Science Diet® pet food.

For an explanation of the symbols used in this section as well as the main directory, please see page 36 or the back flap of this book.

We have provided this list to help you become more familiar with the companies behind popular product names. Please keep in mind, however, that this list is not inclusive of all companies, subsidiaries, divisions and products. And in today's fast-paced business world, subsidiaries, divisions and their brand names are continually being bought and sold. So while this list reflects the most up-to-date information at the time this book went to press, changes may have occurred since then.

The symbol we've assigned to each entry reflects the animal testing policy of the parent company. Because an individual subsidiary may have a different testing policy than its parent company, we suggest that you look up the product listing in the main directory of the book, which begins on page 38, for more specific information.

DNR **3M**

www.3m.com

Products:

Buf-Puf, O-Cel-O, Post-It, Scotch products, Scotch-Brite products, Scotchgard products, Thinsulate

DNR **Advanced Research Laboratories**

www.advreslab.com

Products:

Citre Shine, ClearLogix, got2b, Herbal Logix, Silver Brights, Smooth 'N Shine, Thicker Fuller Hair, Zero Frizz

❤ **Alberto Culver**

www.alberto.com

Subsidiaries/Divisions:

St. Ives Laboratories

Products:

Consort, FDS, Just for Me, Motions, Soft & Beautiful, Static Guard, Swiss Formula, TCB hair products, TRESemme, VO5 products

❤ **Avalon Natural Products**

www.avalonorganics.com

Products:

Alba Botanica, Avalon Organic Botanicals, Avalon Organics, Sonoma Soap Co., Un-petroleum

▼ **Bausch & Lomb Inc.**

www.bausch.com

Products:

Boston products, ReNu Solution, Sensitive Eyes Solution

◆ **Beiersdorf, Inc.**
www.beiersdorf.com
Products:
Curad, Eucerin, Juvena, La Prairie, Nivea

DNR **Bristol-Myers Squibb Co.**
www.bms.com
Products:
Keri

DNR **Chattem, Inc.**
www.chattem.com
Products:
Bull Frog sunblock, Gold Bond, Icy Hot, Mudd, pHisoderm, Selsun Blue,
Sun-in, Ultra Swim

▼ **Church & Dwight Co., Inc.**
www.churchdwight.com
Products:
Aim, Answer Pregnancy and Ovulation Tests, Arm & Hammer, Arrid, Brillo,
Cameo Cleaner, Clean Shower, Close-Up, Delicare, First Response, Fresh'n Clean,
Lady's Choice, Lambert Kay, Mentadent, Nair, Naturalamb Condoms, Parsons'
Ammonia, Pearl Drops, Pepsodent, Rain Drops Water Softener, Scrub Free, Snobol,
Trojan Condoms

▼ Clorox Co.

www.thecloroxcompany.com

Products:

Brita, Clorox products, Combat, EverClean, EverFresh, Formula 409, Fresh Step, Glad products, GladWare, Lestoil, Liquid-Plumr, Pine-Sol, S.O.S., Scoop Away, Soft Scrub, Tilex, Tuffy

▼ Colgate-Palmolive Co.

www.colgate.com

Subsidiaries/Divisions:

Hill's Pet Nutrition

Products:

Afta, Ajax products, Colgate products, Crystal Clean, Crystal White Octagon, Dermassage, Dynamo, Fab products, Irish Spring, Lady Speed Stick, Murphy Oil Soap, Palmolive products, Prescription Diet, Science Diet, Skin Bracer, Softsoap products, Speed Stick, Suavitel, Teen Spirit

▼ Del Laboratories, Inc.

www.dellabs.com

Products:

CornSilk, Gentle Naturals, La Cross, Miss Kiss, N.Y.C. New York Color, Naturistics, Orajel, Pronto, Sally Hansen

▼ Dial Corp., Inc.

www.dialcorp.com

Products:

20 Mule Team, Borateem, Coast, Dial products, Fels Naptha, Pure & Natural, Purex products, Renuzit products, StaFlo starch, Tone, Trend detergent, Zout

❤ Elizabeth Arden, Inc.

www.elizabetharden.com

Products:

Britney Spear's Curious by Britney Spears, Ceramide, Design, Elizabeth Arden 5th Avenue, Elizabeth Arden Green Tea, Elizabeth Arden Provocative Woman, Elizabeth Arden's Red Door, Elizabeth Taylor's Passion, Elizabeth Taylor's White Diamonds, Forever Elizabeth, Gardenia, Geoffrey Beene Grey Flannel, Halston fragrance, Halston Z-14, Millenium, PS Fine Cologne for Men, Red Door Revealed, skinsimple, Sunflowers fragrance, Visible Difference, White Shoulders, Wings fragrance

❤ Estee Lauder Companies

www.elcompanies.com

Brands:

Aramis, Aveda, Bobbi Brown, Bumble and bumble, Clinique, Darphin, Donna Karan Cosmetics, Jo Malone, kate spade beauty, La Mer, MAC, Michael Kors fragrances, Origins, Prescriptives, Rodan+Fields, Stila, Tommy Hilfiger products

▼ Georgia-Pacific

www.gp.com

Products:

Angel Soft, Brawny, Dixie, Green Forest, Mardi Gras, MD, Quilted Northern, So-Dri, Soft 'n Gentle, Sparkle, Vanity Fair, Zee

▼ Gillette Co.

www.gillette.com

Products:

Agility, Atra, Braun, Custom Plus, Daisy, Dry Idea, Duracell, Gillette products, Good News, MACH3 products, Oral-B, Right Guard, Satin Care, Sensor shaving products, Soft & Dri, Trac II, Venus shaving products

▼ GlaxoSmithKline Consumer Healthcare

www.gsk.com
Products:
Aquafresh, Citrucel, Massengill, Nicoderm, Nicorette, Oxy, Polident, Poligrip, Sensodyne

▼ Johnson & Johnson

www.jnj.com
Subsidiaries/Divisions:
Neutrogena Corp., Personal Products Co., RoC S.A.
Products:
Acuvue, Aveeno, Balmex, Band-Aid, Carefree, Clean & Clear, Clean Burst, Healthy Defense, Johnson's Baby Oil, Johnson's Baby Powder, K-Y Brand, Monistat, No More Tears, Norwegian Formula, o.b. Tampons, Rainbath, Reach, Stayfree, T/Gel

◆ Kao Brands Co. (formerly Andrew Jergens Co.)

www.kaobrands.com
Products:
Ban, Beach Blonde, Bioré products, Brilliant Brunette, Curél products, Frizz-Ease, Guhl, Jergens products, John Frieda, Sheer Blonde

▼ Kimberly-Clark Corp.

www.kimberly-clark.com
Products:
Cottonelle, Depend, Good Nites, Huggies, Kleenex, Kotex, Little Swimmers, Neat Sheet, Poise, Pull-Ups, Scott, Viva

◆ L'Oreal

www.loreal.com
Brands:
ARTec, Biotherm, Cacharel, Dermablend, Garnier, Giorgio Armani Parfums, Helena Rubenstein, Kerastase, Kiehl's, La Roche-Posay, Lancome, L'Oreal Paris, Matrix, Maybelline, Mizani, Ombrelle, Paloma Picasso, Ralph Lauren, Redken, Shu Uemura, Softsheen-Carson, Vichy Laboratories

DNR LVMH Moet Hennessy Louis Vuitton

www.lvmh.com
Products:
BeneFit cosmetics, Christian Dior fragrances, Fresh, Givenchy fragrances, Guerlain, Kenzo fragrances

DNR Limited Brands

www.limitedbrands.com
Subsidiaries/Divisions:
Bath & Body Works, Henri Bendel, Inc., Victoria's Secret

DNR Markwins International Corp. (formerly AM Cosmetics, Inc.)

www.markwins.com
Products:
Artmatic cosmetics, Black Radiance cosmetics, Lord & Berry cosmetics, Tropez cosmetics, Wet 'N' Wild cosmetics

DNR **Pfizer**

www.pfizer.com

Products:

Bengay, Corn Huskers lotion, Desitin, E.P.T. Early Pregnancy Test, Efferdent, Fresh 'N Brite toothpaste, Listerine, Listermint, Lubriderm, Pacquin, Plax, Tucks, Visine

DNR **Playtex Products, Inc.**

www.playtexproductsinc.com

Products:

Baby Magic, Banana Boat, Binaca, Mr. Bubble, Ogilvie, Playtex Tampons, Wet Ones, Woolite carpet & laundry cleaners

▼ **Procter & Gamble**

www.pg.com

Subsidiaries/Divisions:

Graham Webb, Sebastian Int'l, Inc., The Iams Company, Wella Corp.

Products:

A Touch of Sun, Alldays, Always, Aussie products, Back to Basics, Balsam Color, Bold, Born Blonde, Bounce, Bounty, Camay, Cascade, Charmin, Cheer, Clairol, Cover Girl, Crest, Daily Defense, Dawn, Downy, Dreft, Dryel, Era, Eukanuba, Febreze, Fixodent, Frost & Tip, Gain, Giorgio Beverly Hills, Gleem, Hairpainting, Head & Shoulders, Herbal Essences, Hugo Boss fragrances, Hydrience, Iams, Infusium 23, Ivory, Ivory Snow, Joy, Lasting Color, Loving Care, Luvs, Max Factor, Men's Choice, Miss Clairol, Mr. Clean, Natural Instincts, Nice 'n Easy, Noxema, Nuances, Ohm by Olay, Olay, Old Spice, Pampers, Pantene, Pert Plus, Physique, Puffs, PUR, Safeguard, Scope, Secret, Sure, Swiffer, Tampax, Thermacare, Tide, Ultress, Vidal Sassoon, Xtah, Zest

▼ Reckitt-Benckiser plc

www.reckittbenckiser.com
Products:
Air Wick, Brasso, Calgon, Easy-Off, Electrasol, Jet-Dry, Lime-A-Way, Lysol, Mop & Glo, O'Cedar, Old English, Resolve, Spray 'n Wash, Veet, Woolite fine fabric wash

❤ Revlon, Inc.

www.revlon.com
Subsidiaries/Divisions:
Almay, Inc.
Products:
Absolutely Fabulous fragrance, Charlie, Fire & Ice fragrance, Flex, Jean Nate, Jeanne Gatineau, Mitchum, Ultima II

▼ S.C. Johnson

www.scjohnson.com
Products:
Armstrong floor cleaner, Brite, Drano, Edge, Fantastik, Future, Glade products, Grab-it, Mr. Muscle, OFF! Products, Oust, Pledge, Raid, Saran, Scrubbing Bubbles, Shout, Skintastic, Skintimate, Toilet Duck, Vanish, Windex, Ziploc products

▼ Schering-Plough Corp.

www.sch-plough.com
Products:
Bain de Soleil, Coppertone, Dr. Scholl's, Lotrimin, Solarcaine, Tinactin

▼ Schwarzkopf & Dep Inc.

www.dep.com

Products:

Agree, Dep, Fa body washes, L.A. Looks, La Perla fragrance, Lavoris, Lilt, Porcelana, Topol toothpaste

▼ Unilever

www.unileverna.com

Brands:

All detergent, Axe deodorant, BCBG Max Azria fragrances, Brut, Calvin Klein fragrances, Caress, Cerruti fragrances, Chloe, Degree, Dove, Final Touch, Finesse, Helene Curtis, Lagerfeld fragrances, Lever 2000, Lever Brothers, Lifebuoy, Lux, Nautica fragrances, Ponds, Q-Tips, Salon Selectives, Shield, Signal Mouthwash, Snuggle, Suave, Sunlight, Surf, ThermaSilk, Valentino fragrances, Vaseline, Vera Wang fragrances, Wisk

CRUELTY-FREE MAIL ORDER COMPANIES

Following is a listing of cruelty-free mail order companies, for those who are having difficulty finding cruelty-free products close by, as well as for those who enjoy the convenience of ordering online, by telephone or by mail.

If you are looking for a particular type of product, such as baby products or fragrances, please refer to the Directory of Cruelty-Free Products by Product Type beginning on page 26 to help you determine which companies sell those products.

Alexandra Avery Purely Natural
4717 SE Belmont
Portland, OR 97215
(800) 669-1863; (503) 236-5926
www.alexandraavery.com
Cosmetics, Personal Care

Allens Naturally
P.O. Box 514
Farmington, MI 48332-0339
(248) 449-7708
www.allensnaturally.com
Household

Amazon Premium Products
275 NE 59th St.
Miami, FL 33137
(800) 832-5645
www.amazonpp.com
Household

Arbonne Int'l
9400 Jeronimo
Irvine, CA 92618
(800) ARBONNE; (949) 770-2610
www.arbonne.com
Cosmetics, Personal Care

Aubrey Organics
4419 N. Manhattan Ave.
Tampa, FL 33614
(800) 282-7394; (813) 877-4186
www.aubrey-organics.com
Companion Animal Care, Cosmetics,
Household, Personal Care

Auromere Ayurvedic Imports
2621 W. Hwy. 12
Lodi, CA 95242
(800) 735-4691; (209) 339-3710
www.auromere.com
Personal Care

Avalon Natural Products
1105 Industrial Ave.
Petaluma, CA 94952
(707) 347-1200
www.avalonorganics.com
Cosmetics, Personal Care

Biogime Skincare, Inc.
25602 I-45 North, Ste. 106
Spring, TX 77386
(800) 338-8784; (281) 298-2607
www.biogimeskincare.com
Cosmetics, Personal Care

Blue Ribbons Pet Care
9 Twin Pine Ln.
Center Moriches, NY 11934
(800) 552-BLUE; (631) 968-9164
www.blueribbonspetcare.com
Companion Animal Care

Body Time
1101 Eighth St., Ste. 100
Berkeley, CA 94710
(510) 524-0216
www.bodytime.com
Personal Care

Clear Conscience, LLC
P.O. Box 17855
Arlington, VA 22216
(800) 595-9592; (703) 527-7566
www.clearconscience.com
Personal Care

Color My Image Inc.
5025B Backlick Rd.
Annadale, VA 22003
(703) 354-9797
www.colormyimage.com
Cosmetics

Earthly Matters
2950 St. Augustine Rd.
Jacksonville, FL 32207
(904) 398-1458
Household

Essential 3 (formerly Jacki's Magic
    Lotion)
145 Hummingbird Ln.
Talent, OR 97540
(800) 355-8428; (541) 535-1866
www.meadowsusa.com
Personal Care

Fleabusters/Rx for Fleas, Inc.
6555 NW 9th Ave., Ste. 412
Fort Lauderdale, FL 33309
(800) 666-3532; (305) 351-9244
www.fleabuster.com
Companion Animal Care, Household

Gerda Spillmann USA
640 Glass Ln.
Modesto, CA 95356
(209) 529-1757
www.gerdaspillmann.com
Cosmetics, Personal Care

Great Mother's Goods
P.O. Box 11425
Syracuse, NY 13218-1425
(800) 984-4848; (315) 476-1385
www.greatmothersgoods.com
Personal Care

Lakon Herbals
720 Templeton Rd.
Montpelier, VT 05602-8584
(802) 223-5563
www.lakonherbals.com
Personal Care

Louise Bianco Skin Care, Inc.
13655 Chandler Blvd.
Sherman Oaks, CA 91401
(800) 782-3067; (818) 786-2700
www.louisebianco.com
Cosmetics, Personal Care

Marilyn Miglin, L.P.
1230 W. Washington Blvd.
Chicago, IL 60607
(800) 322-1133
www.marilynmiglin.com
Cosmetics, Personal Care

Mary Kay Corp.
P.O. Box 799045
Dallas, TX 75379-9045
(800) 627-9529; (972) 687-5577
www.marykay.com
Cosmetics, Personal Care

MediPatch Laboratories Corp.
P.O. Box 795
E. Dennis, MA 02641
(508) 385-4549
www.holisticfamilyandpets.com
Companion Animal Care, Personal Care

Mountain Rose Herbs
P.O. Box 50220
Eugene, OR 97405-8656
(800) 879-3337
www.mountainroseherbs.com
Companion Animal Care, Cosmetics, Personal Care

New Methods
713 S. Main St., #C1
Willits, CA 95490
(707) 456-1262
Companion Animal Care

Orlane, Inc.
555 Madison Ave., 11th Fl.
New York, NY 10022
(212) 750-1111
www.orlaneparis.com
Cosmetics, Personal Care

Pure Touch Therapeutics
P.O. Box 234
Glen Ellen, CA 95442-0234
(800) 442-PURE; (707) 996-7817
www.puretouch.net
Personal Care

Seventh Generation
212 Battery St., Ste. A
Burlington, VT 05401-5232
(802) 658-3773
www.seventhgeneration.com
Household, Personal Care

Simmons Natural Bodycare
42295 Hwy. 36
Bridgeville, CA 95526-9603
(707) 777-1920
www.simmonsnaturals.com
Personal Care

St. John's Herb Garden, Inc.
7711 Hillmeade Rd.
Bowie, MD 20720
(301) 262-5302
www.st-johns.com
Cosmetics, Personal Care

Sunfeather Natural Soap Co.
1551 Hwy. 72
Potsdam, NY 13676
(315) 265-3648
www.sunsoap.com
Companion Animal Care, Personal Care

TARRAH Cosmetics
P.O. Box 243209
Boynton Beach, FL 33424-3209
(561) 374-5995
www.tarrah.com
Cosmetics, Personal Care

TCCD Int'l, Inc.
2301 NW 33rd Ct., Ste. 103
Pompano Beach, FL 33069-1000
(800) 653-4006; (954) 960-4904
www.tccd.com
Personal Care

TerrEssentials
2650 Old National Pike
Middletown, MD 21769-8817
(301) 371-7333
www.terressentials.com
Personal Care

VeganEssentials
3707 N. 92nd St.
Milwaukee, WI 53222
(866) 88-VEGAN; (414) 527-9684
www.veganessentials.com
Companion Animal Care, Cosmetics, Household, Personal Care

Vermont Soapworks
616 Exchange St.
Middlebury, VT 05753-1105
(802) 388-4302
www.vermontsoap.com
Companion Animal Care, Household, Personal Care

Windrose Trading Co.
P.O. Box 990, 108 Schoolhouse Rd.
Madison, VA 22727
(800) 229-3731; (540) 948-2268
www.windrosetrading.com
Personal Care

Wow-Bow Distributors, Ltd.
13 B Lucon Dr.
Deer Park, NY 11729
(800) 326-0230; (631) 254-6064
www.wow-bow.com
Companion Animal Care

Zhen, Inc.
2665 4th Ave. # 102A
Anoka, MN 55303
(800) 457-8455; (763) 323-4817
www.zhenbeauty.com
Cosmetics, Personal Care

Zia Natural Skincare
1337 Evans Ave.
San Francisco, CA 94124
(800) 334-7546; (415) 642-8339
www.zianatural.com
Cosmetics, Personal Care

ANIMAL-DERIVED INGREDIENTS USED IN CONSUMER PRODUCTS

When we designate a product as "cruelty free," we are referring to the fact that neither the product itself, nor the ingredients in it, have been tested on animals. However, some products that have not been tested on animals may contain ingredients that are derived from animals.

Many animal advocates, in addition to avoiding products that are animal-tested, are committed to eliminating products that also contain animal by-products from their daily life, including their diet. These people are called *vegans*. For those who are interested in pursuing the vegan lifestyle, the following list helps clarify the origin of typical ingredients used in the manufacture of food, clothing, cosmetics, personal care and household products.

When referring to this list, it's important to remember that many ingredients can be derived from more than one source—plant, animal or synthetically. Often, it is impossible to tell from the label which source is being used. In that case, you would have to contact the manufacturer to find out the exact origin of the ingredient.

We would like to thank the American Vegan Society for allowing us to reprint their *Listing of Ingredients and Materials: Animal, Vegetable or Mineral?* For more information, contact the American Vegan Society, 56 Dinsha Drive, P.O. Box 369, Malaga, NJ 08328, Tel (856) 694-2887. Or visit their website at www.americanvegan.org.

People for the Ethical Treatment of Animals (PETA) also has a list of animal-derived ingredients. It can be found at www.caringconsumer.com/ingredientsfactsheet.html/.

Ingredients that are always animal derived:

Albumin
Aliphatic Alcohol
Amniotic Fluid
Amylase
Anchovy
Angora
Animal Oils and Fats
Arachidonic Acid
Aspic
Astrakhan
Bee Products
Bee Pollen
Beeswax
Bone Ash
Bone Meal
Bonito Flakes
Brawn
Carmine/Carminic
  Acid
Casein
Cashmere
Castoreum/Castor
(*Different than Castor Oil*)
Catgut
Caviar
Chamois
Chitin
Cholesterin,
Cholesterol
Chole-Calciferol
Civet
Cochineal
Cod Liver Oil
Coral
Down
Duodenum Substances
Egg Albumin
Egg Protein
Eider Down
Elastin
Enzymes
Feathers
Felt
Fish Liver Oil
Fish Scales
Fur
Gelatin
Hide
Hide Glue
Honey
Horsehair
Isinglass
Lactose
Lanolin/Lanol/Lanate
Lard
Leather
Lipase
Luna Sponge
Milk Protein
Mink Oil
Mohair
Musk
Oleoic Oil
Oleostearin
Parchment
Pearl
Pearl, Cultured
Pepsin
Placenta
Polypeptides
Propolis
Quaternium 27
Roe
Royal Jelly
Sable
Shellac
Silk
Sodium 5'-Inosinate
Sperm Oil
Spermaceti Wax
Squalene/Squalane
Suede
Suet
Tallow
Testosterone
Vellum
Whey
Wool

The following ingredients may be derived from an animal, plant or synthetic source. You may have to contact the manufacturer to find out for certain whether an ingredient used in a particular product is derived from animals.

Adrenalin
Allantoin
Ambergris
Amino Acids
Anticaking Agent
Aspartic Acid
Bristle
Calcium Stearate
Caprylic Acid
Caramel
Cetyl Alcohol
Charcoal
Clarifying Agent
Collagen
Coloring
Cortisone/Cortico
  Steroid
Cysteine L-Form,
Cystine
Deoxyribonucleic
  Acid
Emulsifiers
Estrogen
Fatty Acids
Flavorings
Gelling Agent
Glazing Agent
Glucosamine
Glutamic Acid
Glycerides
Glycerin
Guanine
Humectants
Hydrolized Proteins
Insulin
Keratin
L'Cysteine
Hydrochloride
Lactic Acid
Lecithin
Linoleic Acid
Lipoids/Lipids
Lutein
Magnesium Stearate
Natural Source
Nucleic Acid
Nutrients
Oleic Acid
Palmitic Acid
Panthenol
Polypeptides
Progesterone
Proteases
Releasing Agents
Rennet
RNA/DNA
Solvent
Sponge
Stabilizers
Stearates/Stearic Acid
Steroid
Sugar
Urea
Velvet
Vitamin A
Vitamin B12
Vitamin D

HEALTH-BASED CHARITIES THAT DO AND DO NOT FUND ANIMAL RESEARCH

Perhaps you are one of the many people who, in addition to opposing the use of animals in product testing, are also against using animals in biomedical research. Whether you oppose animal research for ethical or scientific reasons—or both—you probably don't want your charitable donations to support not-for-profit organizations that fund animal research.

The following list of charities that DO NOT fund animal research (beginning on page 158) can help you make better informed gift-giving decisions. On page 173, you'll find a list of organizations that DO fund research on animals for the purpose of finding treatments and cures for the diseases on which they are focused.

If you are troubled by the fact that one of your favorite charities funds animal research, you may wish to reconsider who receives your valuable support.

But don't just stop making contributions. Write to that organization and tell them, politely yet firmly, that they will not receive your support until they stop funding animal research.

These two listings represent the most current information available at press time. Changes do occur, so to check the most up-to-date listing, visit www.humaneseal.org. If you do not see your favorite charity on either list, call the Council on Humane Giving at 202-686-2210 or contact them at info@humaneseal.org. To obtain additional information about any of the charities listed, we suggest you call the charity and ask for a written statement regarding their funding policies. If that doesn't work, you can also contact the Council of Better Business Bureaus, Inc. at 703-276-0100.

Photo on facing page: In one experiment using animals, a monkey is forced to smoke a cigarette to get water.

We would like to thank the Council on Humane Giving, of which NAVS is a member, for permission to reprint their listing. The Council on Humane Giving is administered by the Physicians Committee for Responsible Medicine (PCRM), 5100 Wisconsin Avenue, NW, Suite 400, Washington, DC 20016, Tel. 202-686-2210.

This listing does not represent any endorsement by NAVS of any particular organization.

Look for this mark of compassion.

The Humane Charity Seal of Approval

The Humane Charity Seal of Approval helps you easily identify health charities that are committed to funding state-of-the-art research without the use of animals. To receive the Humane Charity Seal, an organization must be approved by the Council on Humane Giving. For more information on the Humane Charity Seal of Approval, go to **www.humaneseal.org**.

CHARITIES THAT DO NOT FUND ANIMAL RESEARCH

AIDS/HIV

AIDS Coalition of Cape Breton
106 Townsend St., Ste. 10
Sydney, NS B1P 6H1
Canada
902-567-1766
www.accb.ns.ca

Caring for Babies with AIDS
5922 Comey Ave.
Los Angeles, CA 90034
323-931-1440

Charlotte HIV/AIDS Network, Inc. (CHAN)
3880 Tamiami Tr., #E
Port Charles, FL 33952
941-625-6650
941-625-AIDS

Chicago House
1925 N. Clayburn,
Ste. 401
Chicago, IL 60614
773-248-5200

Children's Immune Disorder
16888 Greenfield Rd.
Detroit, MI 48235-3707
313-837-7800

Concerned Citizens for Humanity
3580 Main St., Ste. 155
Hartford, CT 06120-1121
860-560-0833

Design Industries Foundation Fighting AIDS (DIFFA)
147 W. 24th St., Fl. 7
New York, NY 10011
212-727-3100
www.diffa.org

Health Cares Exchange Initiative, Inc.
7100 N. Ashland Ave.
Chicago, IL 60626
617-499-7780
www.hcei.org

HIV Network of Edmonton Society
10550-102 St.
Edmonton, AB T5H 2T3
Canada
780-488-5742
780-488-3735

Joshua Tree Feeding Program, Inc.
1601 W. Indian School Rd.
Pheonix, AZ 85015-5223
602-264-0223

Loving Arms
P.O. Box 3368
Memphis, TN 38173
901-725-6730

Miracle House of New York
80 Eighth Ave., Ste. 709
New York, NY 10011
212-989-7790
www.miraclehouse.org

Phoenix Shanti Group, Inc.
2020 W. Indian School Rd.,
#50
Phoenix, AZ 85015
602-279-0008

Puerto Rico Community Network for Clinical Research on AIDS
P.O. Box 20850
San Juan, PR 00928-0850
809-753-9443

ARTHRITIS

Arthritis Research Institute of America
300 S. Duncan Ave., Ste. 240
Clearwater, FL 33755
727-461-4054
www.preventarthritis.org

Arthritis Trust of America
7111 Sweetgum Rd., Ste. A
Fairview, TN 37062-9384
615-799-1002
www.arthritistrust.org

BIRTH DEFECTS

Birth Defect Research for Children
930 Woodcock Rd., Ste. 225
Orlando, FL 32803
800-313-2232
www.birthdefects.org

Easter Seal Society
1185 Eglington Ave. E., Ste. 706
Toronto, ON M3C 3C6
Canada
800-668-6252
416-696-1035

Easter Seals
230 W. Monroe St., Ste. 1800
Chicago, IL 60606
800-221-6827
www.easter-seals.org

Little People's Research Fund, Inc.
80 Sister Pierre Dr.
Towson, MD 21204
800-232-5773
www.lprf.org

National Craniofacial Association
P.O. Box 11082
Chattanooga, TN 37401
800-332-2373
www.faces-cranio.org

Puerto Rico Down Syndrome Foundation
P.O. Box 195273
San Juan, PR 00919-5273
787-287-2800

Spina Bifida Association of America
4590 MacArthur Blvd., N.W., Ste. 250
Washington, DC 20007
800-621-3141
www.sbaa.org

Warner House
1023 E. Chapman Ave.
Fullerton, CA 92831
714-441-2600
www.warnerhouse.com

BLIND/DEAF

American Association of the Deaf-Blind
814 Thayer Ave., Ste. 302
Silver Spring, MD 20910

Deaf-Blind Service Center
2366 Eastlake Ave., E., Ste. 206
Seattle, WA 98102
206-323-9178

BLIND/VISUALLY IMPAIRED

American Action Fund for Blind Children and Adults
1800 Johnson St.
Baltimore, MD 21230
410-659-9315
www.actionfund.org

The list of charities that DO fund animal research begins on page 173.

Collier County Association for the Blind
4701 Golden Gate Pkwy.
Naples, FL 34116
239-649-1122
www.naples.net/social/ccab

Connecticut Institute for the Blind/Oak Hill
120 Holcomb St.
Hartford, CT 06112-1589
860-242-2274
www.ciboakhill.org

Foundation for the Junior Blind
5200 Angeles Vista Blvd.
Los Angeles, CA 90043
323-295-4555
www.fjb.org

Helen Keller Worldwide
352 Park Ave. S., Ste. 1200
New York, NY 10010
877-535-5374
www.hkworld.org

International Eye Foundation
10801 Connecticut Ave.
Kensington, MD 20895
240-290-0263
www.iefusa.org

Living Skills Center for Visually Impaired
2430 Rd. 20 Apt.112
Towson, MD 21204
510-234-4984

National Association for the Visually Handicapped
22 W. 21st St., 6th Fl.
New York, NY 10010
212-255-2804
www.navh.org

National Federation of the Blind
1800 Johnson St., Ste. 300
Baltimore, MD 21230
410-659-9314
www.nfb.org

Radio Information Service
2100 Wharton St.,
Ste. 140
Pittsburgh, PA 15203
412-488-3944
www.readingservice.org

Visions Resource Center
1414 Bragg Blvd.
Fayetteville, NC 28303
910-483-2719

VISIONS/Services for the Blind and Visually Impaired
500 Greenwich St.,
3rd Floor
New York, NY 10013-1354
212-625-1616
www.visionsvcb.org

Washington Volunteer Readers for the Blind
901 G St., N.W.
Washington, DC 20001
202-727-2142

BLOOD

Canadian Red Cross
(Croix-Rouge canadienne)
National Office
170 Metcalfe St., Ste. 300
Ottowa, ON K2P 2P2
Canada
613-740-1900
613-740-1911
www.redcross.ca

Michigan Community Blood Centers
P.O. Box 1704
Grand Rapids, MI 49501
1-866-MIBLOOD
www.miblood.org

BURNS

Children's Burn Foundation
4929 Van Nuys Blvd.
Sherman Oaks, CA 91403
818-907-2822

CANCER

American Breast Cancer Foundation
1055 Taylor Ave., Ste. 201
Baltimore, MD 21286
410-825-9388
www.abcf.org

AP John Institute for Cancer Research
67 Arch St.
Greenwich, CT 6830
203-661-2571
www.apjohncancerinsti-tute.org

Avon Breast Cancer Crusade
Avon Products
Foundation, Inc.
1345 Avenue of the Americas
New York, NY 10105
877-WALKAVON
www.avoncrusade.com

Breast Cancer Fund
2107 O'Farrell St.
San Francisco, CA 94115
415-346-8223

Calvary Fund, Inc.
1740 Eastchester Rd.
Bronx, NY 10461
877-4-CALVARY
www.calvaryhospital.org

Cancer Care Services
605 W. Magnolia
Fort Worth, TX 76104
817-921-0653

Cancer Fund of America, Inc.
2901 Breezewood Ln.
Knoxville, TN 37921-1099
800-441-1664
www.cfoa.org

Cancer Project
5100 Wisconsin Ave., N.W., Ste. 400
Washington, DC 20016
202-686-2210
www.cancerproject.org

Cancer Treatment Research Foundation
3150 Salt Creek Ln., Ste. 122
Arlington Heights, IL 60005-1087
847-342-7443
847-342-7461
www.ctrf.org

Danville Cancer Association, Inc.
1225 W. Main St.
P.O. Box 2148
Danville, VA 24541
434-792-3700

Garland Appeal
39 W. 54th St.
New York, NY 10019
1728454820
www.garlandappeal.com

Gilda Radner Familial Ovarian Cancer Registry
Roswell Park 18 Institute
Elm & Carlton Sts.
Buffalo, NY 14263-0001
800-682-7426

Lymphoma Foundation of America
814 N. Garfield St.
Arlington, VA 22201
703-875-9800
www.lymphomahelp.org

National Children's Cancer Society
1015 Locust, Ste. 1040
Saint Louis, MO 63101
314-241-1600

Quest Cancer Research
Seedbed Business Centre,
Unit E3
Coldharbour Rd.,
Pinnacles E.
Harlow, Essex CM19 5AF
United Kingdom
1279451359

Share
1501 Broadway, Ste. 101
New York, NY 10036
866-891-2392
212-869-3431
www.sharecancersupport.org

Skin Cancer Foundation
245 Fifth Ave., Ste. 1403
New York, NY 10016
800-754-6490

Tomorrows Children's Fund
Hackensack University
Medical Center
30 Prospect Ave.
Hackensack, NJ 7601
201-996-5500
www.atcfkid.com

United Cancer Research Society
3545 20th St.
Highland, CA 92346-4542
800-222-1533
www.unitedcancer.org

CARDIOVASCULAR

American Pediatric Heart Fund
16024 Manchester Rd.,
Ste. 200
Saint Louis, MO 63011
636-594-2202
636-594-2210
www.aphfund.org

Lown Cardiovascular Center
21 Longwood Ave.
Brookline, MA 2446
617-732-1318
www.lowncenter.org

CHILDREN'S HEALTH

Children's Cancer Association
7524 S.W. Macadam, Ste. B
Portland, OR 97219
503-244-3141
www.childrenscancerassociation.org

Children's Diagnostic Center, Inc.
2100 Pleasant Ave.
Hamilton, OH 45015
513-868-1562

Children's Health Environmental Coalition
P.O. Box 1540
Princeton, NJ 08542
609-252-1915
www.checnet.org

Children's Wish Foundation International
8615 Roswell Rd.
Atlanta, GA 30350-4867
800-323-WISH
www.childrenswish.org

Five Acres/The Boys' and Girls' Aid Society of Los Angeles
760 W. Mountain View St.
Altadena, CA 91001
626-798-6793
www.5acres.org

Floating Hospital
Pier 11, E. River at Wall St.
New York, NY 10005
212-514-7440
www.thefloatinghospital.org

Healing Species
P.O. Box 1202
Orangeburg, SC 29116
803-535-6543
www.healingspecies.org

Miracle Flights
2756 N. Green Valley
Pkwy., Ste. 115
Green Valley, NV 89014
702-261-0494
www.miracleflights.org

MISS Foundation
P.O. Box 5333
Peoria, AZ 85385-5333
623-979-1000
www.missfoundation.org

Pathfinder International
9 Galen St., Ste. 217
Watertown, MA 02172
617-924-7200

Rainbow Society of Alberta
6604 82nd Ave.
Edmonton, AB T6B 0E7
Canada
780-469-3306
http://rainbowsociety.ab.ca

DEAF/HEARING IMPAIRED

Better Hearing Institute
515 King St., Ste. 420
Alexandria, VA 22314
703-684-3391
www.betterhearing.org

Chicago Hearing Society
2001 W. Clybourn Ave.
Chicago, IL 60614
773-248-9121
www.chicagohearingsoci-ety.org

Deaf Action Center
3115 Crestview Dr.
Dallas, TX 75235
214-521-0407
www.deafactioncenter-texas.org

Deaf Independent Living Association, Inc.
P.O. Box 4038
Salisbury, MD 21803
410-742-5052
www.dila.org

Deaf Service Center of St. Johns County
207 San Marco Ave., #380
Saint Augustine, FL
32084-2762

Dogs for the Deaf, Inc.
10175 Wheeler Rd.
Central Point, OR 97502
541-826-9220
www.dogsforthedeaf.org

Institute for Rehabilitation, Research, and Recreation, Inc.
P.O. Box 1025
Pendelton, OR 97801
541-276-2752

League for the Hard of Hearing
71 W. 23rd St.
New York, NY 10010
917-305-7800
www.lhh.org

Minnesota State Academy for the Deaf
P.O. Box 308
Faribault, MN 55021
507-332-5402
www.msad.state.mn.us

DISABLED, DEVELOPMENTALLY

Achievements, Inc.
101 Mineral Ave.
Libby, MT 59923
406-293-8848

Adult Activity Services
307 E. Atlantic St.
Emporia, VA 23847
434-634-2124

Adult Training and Habilitation Center
311 Fairlawn Ave., W.
P.O. Box 600
Winsted, MN 55395
320-485-4191

American Association on Mental Retardation
444 N. Capitol St., N.W., Ste. 846
Washington, DC 20001
800-424-3688
www.aamr.org

Association for Community Living
One Carando Dr.
Springfield, MA 01104
413-732-0531

Burnt Mountain Center
P.O. Box 337
Jasper, GA 30143
706-692-6016

Butler Valley, Inc.
380 12th St.
Arcata, CA 95521
707-822-0301

Career Development Center
2110 W. Delaware
Fairfield, IL 62837
618-842-2691

Carroll Haven Achieving New Growth Experiences
115 Stoner Ave.
Westminister, MD 21157
410-876-2179

Christian Horizons
384 Arthur St. S.
Elmira, ON N3B 2P4
Canada
519-669-1571

Community Services
452 Delaware Ave.
Buffalo, NY 14202-1515
716-883-8888

Concerned Citizens for the Developmentally Disabled/Community Options
801B Washington St.
P.O. Box 725
Chillicothe, MO 64601
660-646-0109

Dewitt County Human Resource Center
1150 Rte. 54 W.
Clinton, IL 61727
217-935-9496

Eagle Valley Children's Home
2300 Eagle Valley Ranch Rd.
Carson City, NV 89703
775-882-1188

EYAS Corporation
411 Scarlet Sage St.
Punta Gorda, FL 33950
941-575-2255

Hartville Meadows
P.O. Box 1055
Hartville, OH 44632
330-877-3694

Hebron Community, Inc.
P.O. Box 11
Lawrenceville, VA 23868

Hope House Foundation
801 Boush St., Ste. 302
Norfolk, VA 23510
757-625-6161
www.hope-house.org

Horizons Specialized Services, Inc.
405 Oak St.
Steamboat Springs, CO 80477-4867
973-879-4466

Kensington Community Corporation for Individual Dignity
5425 Oxford Ave.
Philadelphia, PA 19124
215-288-9797

Mountain Valley Developmental Services
P.O. Box 338
Glenwood Springs, CO 81602
970-945-2306

Mt. Angel Training Center and Residential Services
350 E. Church St.
Mt. Angel, OR 97362
503-845-9214

New Oppurtunities
1400 Seventh St.
Madison, IL 62060
618-876-3178

Nia Comprehensive Center for Developmental Disabilities
1808 S. State St.
Chicago, IL 60616
312-949-1808
800-NIA-1976

Opportunities Unlimited
3340 Marysville Blvd.
Sacramento, CA 95838
716-297-6400

Orange County Association for the Help of Retarded Citizens
249 Broadway
Newburgh, NY 12550
914-561-0670

Outlook Nashville, Inc.
3004 Tuggle Ave.
Nashville, TN 37211
615-834-7570

Phoenix Services, Inc.
221 W. Penn Ave.
Cleona, PA 10742
717-228-0400

Pleasant View Homes, Inc.
P.O. Box 426
Broadway, VA 22815
540-896-8255

Primrose Center
2733 S. Fern Creek Ave.
Orlando, FL 32806-5591
407-898-7201

RocVale Children's Home
4450 N. Rockton Ave.
Rockford, IL 61103
815-654-3050

San Antonio State School
P.O. Box 14700
San Antonio, TX 78241
210-532-9610

Society to Aid Retarded, Inc. (S.T.A.R.)
P.O. Box 1075
Torrance, CA 90505

Southwest Human Development
202 E. Earll Dr., Ste. 140
Pheonix, AZ 85012
602-266-5976

St. Joseph Home, Inc.
1226 S. Sunbury Rd.
Westerville, OH 43081

Swift County Developmental Achievement Center
2135 Minnesota Ave., Bldg. 1
Benson, MN 56215
320-843-4201

DISABLED, PHYSICALLY

A+ Home Care, Inc.
8932 Old Cedar Ave S.
Bloomington, MN 55425
800-603-7760

Access to Independence, Inc.
2345 Atwood Ave.
Madison, WI 53704-560
608-242-8484

Association for Persons with Physical Disabilities of Windsor and Essex Counties
2001 Spring Garden Rd.
Windsor, ON N9E 3P8
Canada
519-969-8188

Friends
27 Forest St.
Parry Sound, ON
P2A 2R2
Canada
705-746-5102

Hamilton District Society for Disabled Children
Box 200, Station A
Sanitorium Rd.
Hamilton, ON L8N 3Z5
Canada
905-385-5391

Handicapped Housing Society of Alberta
205 - 3132 Parsons Rd.
Edmonton, AB T6N 1L6
Canada
780-451-1114

Independence Crossroads, Inc.
8932 Old Cedar Ave. S.
Bloomington, MN 55425
952-854-8004

Michigan Wheelchair Athletic Association
P.O. Box 1455
Troy, MI 48099
810-977-6123

Mower Council for the Handicapped, Inc.
111 N. Main St.
Austin, MN 55912-3404
507-433-9609

N.W.T. Council for Disabled Persons
P.O. Box 1387
Yellowknife, NT X1A 2P1
Canada
867-873-8230

Southwestern Independent Living Center
843 N. Main St.
Jamestown, NY 14701
716-661-3010

Special People, Inc.
1420 Miner St., City Hall
Des Plaines, IL 60016

Tobias House Attendant Care, Inc.
695 Coxwell Ave., Ste. 611
Toronto, ON M4C 5R6
Canada
416-690-3185
www.tobiashouse.ca

United Amputee Services
P.O. Box 4277
Winter Park, FL 37793
407-359-5500
www.oandp.com/resources/organizations/uasa/

DISABLED, PHYSICALLY OR DEVELOPMENTALLY

Be an Angel Fund
5840 San Felipe
Houston, TX 77057
713-917-3568

Cheyenne Village, Inc.
6275 Lehman Dr.
Colorado Springs, CO 80918
941-625-6650

Comprehensive Advocacy, Inc.
4477 Emerald, Ste. B100
Boise, ID 83706-2044
800-632-5125

Disability Rights Education & Defense Fund (DREDF)
2212 Sixth St.
Berkeley, CA 94710
510-644-2555

Disabled Resource Services
424 Pine St., Ste. 101
Fort Collins, CO 80524
970-482-2700

Families Helping Families at the Crossroads of Louisiana
818 Main St., Ste. A
Pineville, LA 71360
800-259-7200
800-259-7200

Heartland Opportunity Center
Madera Center, 323 N.E. St.
Madera, CA 93638-3245
559-674-8828

Hodan Center, Inc.
941 W. Fountain St.
P.O. Box 212
Mineral Point, WI 53565
608-987-3336

Humboldt Community Access and Resource Center
P.O. Box 2010
Eureka, CA 95502

Indiana Rehabilitation Association
P.O. Box 44174
Indianapolis, IN 46244
317-290-4320

Kinsmen Telemiracle Foundation
2217C Hanselman Ct., #C
Saskatoon, SK S7L 6A8
Canada
877--777-8979
telemiracle@sasktel.net

Lifegains, Inc.
1601 S. Sterling St.
P.O. Drawer 1559
Morganton, NC 28680
704-255-8845

Maidstone Foundation, Inc.
1225 Broadway
New York, NY 10001
828-433-7498

North Country Center for Independence
102 Sharron Ave.
Plattsburgh, NY 12901
518-563-9058

Options Center for Independent Living
22 Heritage Plz., Ste. 107
Boubonnais, IL 60914
815-936-0100

Ozarks Valley Community Service, Inc. (OVCS)
135 S. Main
Ironton, MO 63650-0156
573-546-2418

Rehabilitation Center
1439 Buffalo St.
Olean, NY 14760
716-372-8909

Rehabilitation Society of Calgary
#7, 11th St., N.E.
Calgary, AB T2E 4Z2
Canada
rehabcalgary@shaw.ca
www.members.shaw.ca/rehab-calgary/rehabcalgary.html

Resource Center for Accessible Living, Inc.
602 Albany Ave.
Kingston, NY 12401
845-331-0541

Riverfront Foundation
944 Green Bay St.
La Crosse, WI 54601
608-784-9450

Rockingham Opportunities
342 Cherokee Camp Rd.
Reidsville, NC 27320
336-342-4761

Sheltered Workshop
P.O. Box 2002
Clarksburg, WV 26302
304-623-3757

Society for Handicapped Citizens
4283 Paradise Rd.
Seville, OH 44273
330-725-7041

Southwest Center for Independent Living
2864 S. Nettleton Ave.
Springfield, MO 65807
800-676-7245

Specialized Training for Adult Rehabilitation (START)
20 N. 13th St.
Murphysboro, IL 62966
618-687-2378

St. Paul Abilities Network
P.O. Box 457
4915-51 Ave.
St. Paul, AB T0A 3A0
Canada
866-645-3900
780-645-1885
mail@spanet.ab.ca
www.stpaulabilitiesnetwork.ca

Turn Community Services
P.O. Box 1287
Salt Lake City, UT 84110
866-359-8876

Victor C. Neumann Association
5547 N. Ravenswood St.
Chicago, IL 60640
773-769-4313
www.vcna.org

Vocational Services, Inc.
935 Kent St.
Liberty, MO 64068
816-781-6292

VOLAR Center for Independent Living
8929 Viscount, Ste. 101
El Paso, TX 79225
915-591-0800
volar1@whc.net

Waukesha Training Center
300 S. Prairie
Waukesha, WI 53186
414-547-6821

Western Carolina Center Foundation, Inc.
P.O. Box 646
Morganton, NC 28680
704-433-2862

Workshop/Northeast Career Planning
339 Broadway
Menards, NY 12204
518-273-0818

ELDERLY

Aging & Disabled Services, Inc.
811 S. Palmer Ave.,
Box 142
Georgiana, AL 36033
Beth Haven
2500 Pleasant St.
Hannibal, MO 63401
573-221-6000

Carroll County Health and Home Care Services
Carroll County Complex
Osipee, NH 3864
800-499-4171

DARTS
1645 Marthaler Ln. W.
St. Paul, MN 55118
651-422-1560

Getabout
P.O. Box 224
New Canaan, CT 06840
203-972-7433

Prairie Mission Retirement Village
242 Carroll St. R.R. 1,
Box 1Z
St. Paul, KS 66771
620-449-2400

**Royal Freemasons'
Benevolent Institution
of NSW**
P.O. Box A 2019
Sydney South, NSW 2000
Australia
011 612 9264 59

Wesley Heights
580 Long Hill Ave.
Shelton, CT 6484
203-929-5396

EMOTIONAL/
BEHAVIORAL
DISORDERS

AIM Center
1903 McCallie Ave.
Chattanooga, TN 37404
423-624-4800

Burke Foundation
20800 Farm Rd. 150 W.
Driftwood, TX 78619
512-858-4258

**Crestwood Children's
Center**
2075 Scottsville Rd.
Rochester, NY 14623
716-436-4442
www.hillside.com

**Federation of Families for
Children Mental Health**
1101 King St., Ste. 402
Alexandria, VA 22314
703-684-7710
www.ffcmh.org

Grace House
2412 Tulip
Carlsbad, NM 88220
505-885-3681
www.gracehouse.net

Lake Whatcom Center
3400 Agate Hts.
Bellingham, WA 98226
360-676-6000

**Parents and Children
Coping Together**
P.O. Box 26691
Richmond, VA 23261
804-559-6833
800-477-0946
www.pacct.net

Rimrock Foundation
1231 N. 29th St.
Billings, MT 59101
800-227-3953

**Staten Island Mental
Health Society, Inc.**
669 Castleton Ave.
Staten Island, NY 10301
718-442-2225

**Timberlawn Psychiatric
Research Foundation,
Inc.**
P.O. Box 270789
Dallas, TX 75227-0789
214-338-0451

**TRANSACT Health
Systems of Central
Pennsylvania**
610 Beatty Rd.
Monroeville, PA 15146
814-371-0414

**Youth Services for
Oklahoma County**
21 N.E. 50th St.
Oklahoma City, OK
73105-1811
405-235-7537

HOME CARE/
MEALS

**American Hospice
Foundation**
2120 L St., N.W. , Ste. 200
Washington, DC 20037
202-223-0204
www.americanhospice.org

**Bronx Home Care
Services, Inc.**
3956 Bronxwood Ave.
Bronx, NY 10466
718-231-6292

Greystoke Homes and Support Services, Inc.
701-2 Avenue S.
Lethbridge, AB T1J 0C4
Canada
403-320-0911
403-320-0955

Mobile Meals, Inc.
1063 S. Broadway
Akron, OH 44311
330-376-7717
www.mobilemealsinc.org

Project Open Hand
730 Polk St.
San Francisco, CA 94109
415-477-2300
www.openhand.org

KIDNEY

American Kidney Fund
6110 Executive Blvd., Ste. 1010
Rockville, MD 20852
800-638-8299
www.kidneyfund.org

MISCELLANEOUS

AFAAR
175 W. 12th St., #16-G
New York, NY 10011
212-989-8073

American Leprosy Missions
One ALM Way
Greenville, SC 29601
800-543-3135
www.leprosy.org

American Vitiligo Research Foundation
P.O. Box 7540
Clearwater, FL 33758
727-461-3899
www.avrf.org

Autism Treatment Services of Saskatchewan, Inc.
229 Avenue C N.
Saskatoon, SK S7L 5Z2
Canada
306-655-7013

Colostomy Society of New York
Box 517
New York, NY 10016
212-903-4713

Giving MD a Voice — Committee of Hope and Awareness for Muscular Dystrophy
5334 Granada Blvd.
Sebring, FL 33872
866-632-8642

Healing Hands Project
P.O. Box 1057
Burbank, CA 91507-9998
323-851-2000
www.healinghandsproject.com

Heimlich Institute
P.O. Box 8858
Cincinnati, OH 45208
513-559-2391
www.heimlichinstitute.org

Lions Eye Bank of PA, Inc.
5015 Richmond St.
Erie, PA 16509-1949
814-866-3545

MAWA Trust
66 Oxford St., Ste. 6A
Darlinghurst, NSW 2010
Australia
29360.7114

McDougall Research and Education Foundation
P.O. Box 14309
Santa Rosa, CA 95402
707-538-8609
www.drmcdougall.com

MCS Referral and Resources (Multiple Chemical Sensitivity)
508 Westgate Rd.
Baltimore, MD 21229
410-362-6400
www.mcsrr.org

Multiple Sclerosis Foundation
6350 N. Andrews Ave.
Fort Lauderdale, FL
33309-2130
954-776-6805

National Stuttering Project
5100 E. LaPalma Ave.,
Ste. 208
Anaheim Hills, CA 92807
714-693-7480

Naturaleza, Inc.
8889 Mentor Ave.
Mentor, OH 44060
440-796-6319
www.naturalezafounda-tion.org

Seva Foundation
1786 Fifth St.
Berkeley, CA 94710
510-845-7382
www.seva.org

Thyroid Society
7515 S. Main St., Ste. 545
Houston, TX 77030
800-THYROID

Transplantation Society of Michigan
2203 Platt Rd.
Ann Arbor, MI 48104
800-482-4881
www.tsm-giftoflife.org

PARALYSIS

Follow-Your-Heart Foundation
5144 Bascule Ave.
Woodland Hills, CA
91364-3447
818-992-3212

Spinal Cord Injury Network International
3911 Princeton Dr.
Santa Rosa, CA 95405
800-548-CORD
www.spinalcordinjury.org

STROKE

Palm Springs Stroke Activity Center
2800 E. Alejo St.
P.O. Box 355
Palm Springs, CA 92263
760-323-7676

Stroke Survivors Support Group of Pueblo
710 1/2 E.Mesa Ave.
Pueblo, CO 81006
719-583-8498

SUBSTANCE ABUSE

Family Service Association
31 W. Market St.
Wilkes-Barre, PA 18701
570-823-5144

Friendly Hand Foundation
347 S. Normandie Ave.
Los Angeles, CA 90020
213-389-9964

Prevention of Alcohol Problems
2125 Glenhaven Ln. N.
Brooklyn Park, MN
55443-3806
612-729-3047

Pride Youth Programs
4 W. Oak St.
Fremont, MI 49412
800-668-9277
www.prideyouthpro-grams.org

Samaritan Recovery Community, Inc.
319 S. Fourth St.
Nashville, TN 37206
615-244-4802

TRAUMA/ INJURY

Brain Injury Association of America
105 N. Alfred St.
Alexandria, VA 22314
703-236-6000
www.biausa.org

Brain Injury Association of Florida, Inc.
201 E. Sample Rd.
Pompano Beach, FL 33064
954-786-2400
www.biaf.org

Brain Injury Rehabilitation Centre
300, 815 - 8th Ave., S.W.
Calgary, AB T2P 3P2
Canada
403-297-0100
403-234-8860
birc@brainrehab.ca
http://www.brainrehab.ca/

Trauma Foundation
1001 Potrero Ave., Bldg. 1, Rm. 300
San Francisco, CA 94110
415-821-8209
www.tf.org

VETERANS' HEALTH

Help Hospitalized Veterans
36585 Penfield Ln.
Winchester, CA 92596
909-926-4500

CHARITIES THAT DO FUND ANIMAL RESEARCH

ALZHEIMER'S DISEASE

Alzheimer's Association
919 N. Michigan Ave., Ste. 1000
Chicago, IL 60611-1676
800-272-3900
312-335-8700
info@alz.org
www.alz.org

Alzheimer's Disease Research
American Health Assistance Foundation
15825 Shady Grove Rd., Ste. 140
Rockville, MD 20850
800-437-AHAF
ghandiboe@ahaf.org
www.ahaf.org

AIDS/HIV

American Foundation for AIDS Research
120 Wall St., 13th Fl.
New York, NY 10005
800-39-amFAR
212-806-1601
www.amfar.org

City of Hope
1500 E. Duarte Rd.
Duarte, CA 91010
800-826-HOPE
626-359-8111

Elizabeth Glazer Pediatric AIDS Foundation
2950 31st St., #125
Santa Monica, CA 90405
888-499-4673
310-314-1459
info@pedaids.org
www.pedaids.org

Pediatric AIDS Foundation
1311 Colorado Ave.
Santa Monica, CA 90405
310-395-9051

BIRTH DEFECTS

March of Dimes Birth Defects Foundation
1275 Mamaroneck Ave.
White Plains, NY 10605
888-663-4637
914-997-4504

United Cerebral Palsy
1660 L St., N.W., Ste. 700
Washington, DC 20036
202-776-0406
ucpnatl@ucpa.org

BLOOD

American Red Cross
2025 E St., N.W.
Washington, DC 20006
800-435-7669
202-303-4498
info@usa.redcross.org
www.redcross.org

Aplastic Anemia & MDS International Foundation, Inc.
P.O. Box 316
Annapolis, MD 21404
800-747-2820
help@aamds.org
www.aamds-international.org

National Hemophilia Foundation
116 W. 32nd St., 11th Fl.
New York, NY 10001
800-424-2634
212-328-3777
development@hemophilia.org

CANCER

American Brain Tumor Association
2727 River Rd., Ste. 146
Des Plains, IL 60018-4110
800-886-2282
info@abta.org
www.abta.org

American Cancer Society
1599 Clifton Rd., N.E.
Atlanta, GA 30329
404-320-3333

American Institute for Cancer Research
1759 R St., N.W.
Washington, DC 20009
800-843-8114
202-328-7226
aicrweb@aicr.org

Arizona Cancer Center
1515 N. Campbell Ave.
P.O. Box 245013
Tucson, AZ 85724-5013
800-327-CURE
www.azcc.arizona.edu/who
s_who/w_dorr.htm

Breast Cancer Research Foundation
654 Madison Ave.,
Ste. 1209
New York, NY 10021
646-497-2600
bcrf@estee.com
www.bcrfcure.org

Cancer Research Foundation of America
1600 Duke St., Ste. 110
Alexandria, VA 22314
800-227-2732
703-836-4412
jandahazy@crfa.org
www.preventcancer.org

Childrens Cancer Research Fund
4930 W. 77th St.,
Ste. 364
Minneapolis, MN 55435
952-893-9355
800-4CCRF48

City of Hope
1500 E. Duarte Rd.
Duarte, CA 91010
800-826-HOPE
626-359-8111

Dana Farber Cancer Institute
44 Binney St.
Boston, MA 02115
866-408-DFCI
www.dfci.harvard.edu

Fred Hutchinson Cancer Research Center
1100 Fairview Ave. N.,
P.O. Box 19024
Seattle, WA 98109
206-667-5000
www.fhcrc.org

G&P Foundation for Cancer Research
770 Lexington Ave.,
16th Fl.
New York, NY 10021
212-486-2575
www.gpfoundation.com

The Jimmy Fund
375 Longwood Ave. W.
Boston, MA 02215-7295
800-52-JIMMY
info@jimmyfund.org

The Jimmy V Foundation
100 Towerview Ct.
Cary, NC 27513
919-380-9505
800-4-JIMMYV
info@jimmyv.org
www.jimmyv.org

John Wayne Cancer Center Institute
at Saint John's Hospital and Health Center
2200 Santa Monica Blvd.
Santa Monica, CA 90404
800-262-6259
310-315-6111
jwci@jwci.org
www.jwci.org

The Leukemia and Lymphoma Society
1311 Mamaroneck Ave.
White Plains, NY 10605
914-949-5213
www.leukemia.org

Lombardi Cancer Center
New Research Bldg.,
Room E501
3970 Reservoir Rd., N.W.
Washington, DC 20007
202-687-2956

Memorial Sloan-Kettering Cancer Center
1275 York Ave.
New York, NY 10021
212-639-2000
publicaffairs@mskcc.org

National Cancer Coalition
757 St. Charles Ave.,
Ste. 202
New Orleans, LA 70130

National Cancer Research Center (Walker Cancer Institute)
18 N. Law St.
Aberdeen, MD 21001
410-272-0775

National Colorectal Cancer Research Alliance
(Entertainment Industry Foundation)
11132 Ventura Blvd., #401
Studio City, CA 91604
818-760-7722
www.eifoundation.org

National Foundation for Cancer Research
4600 East-West Hwy.
Bethesda, MD 20814
800-321-2873

National Women's Cancer Research Alliance
(Entertainment Industry Foundation)
11132 Ventura Blvd.,
Ste. 401
Studio City, CA 91604
818-760-7722
www.eifoundation.org

Nina Hyde Center for Breast Cancer Research
(Lombardi Cancer Research Center)
3800 Reservoir Rd., N.W.
Washington, DC 20007
202-687-4597

Ovarian Cancer Research Fund
One Penn Plaza,
Ste. 1610
New York, NY 10119
212-268-1002
800-873-5969
www.ocrf.org

Susan G. Komen Breast Cancer Foundation
5005 LBJ Freeway,
Ste. 250
Dallas, TX 75244
800-462-9273
972-855-1600
education@komen.org
www.komen.org

The V Foundation for Cancer Research
(The Jimmy V Foundation)
100 Towerview Ct.
Cary, NC 27513
919-380-9505
800-4-JIMMYV
info@jimmyv.org
www.jimmyv.org

CARDIOVASCULAR

American Heart Assn
7272 Greenville Ave.
Dallas, TX 75231-4596
800-242-8721
214-373-6300
ncrp@heart.org

Heart and Stroke Foundation of Canada
222 Queen St., Ste. 1402
Ottowa, ON K1P 5V9
Canada
613-569-4361
www.hsf.ca

National Cardiovascular Research Initiative
(Entertainment Industry Foundation)
11132 Ventura Blvd.,
Ste. 401
Studio City, CA 91604
818-760-7722
www.eifoundation.org

National Heart Foundation
(American Health Assistance Foundation)
15825 Shady Grove Rd.,
Ste. 140
Rockville, MD 20850
800-437-AHAF

National Stroke Association
9707 E. Easter Ln.
Englewood, CO 80112
800-STROKES
303-649-9299

CHILDREN'S HEALTH

Boys Town National Research Hospital
555 N. 30th St.
Omaha, NE 68131
402-498-6511

Childrens Cancer Research Fund
4930 W. 77th St.,
Ste. 364
Minneapolis, MN 55435
952-893-9355
800-4CCRF48

Childrens Hospital of Pittsburgh Foundation
3705 Fifth Ave.
Pittsburgh, PA 15213
412-692-7436
www.chp.edu

Children's Miracle Network
4525 South 2300 East,
Ste. 202
Salt Lake City, UT 84117
801-278-8900
801-277-8787
www.cmn.org

Elizabeth Glazer Pediatric AIDS Foundation
2950 31st St., #125
Santa Monica, CA 90405
888-499-4673
310-314-1459
info@pedaids.org
www.pedaids.org

The Leukemia and Lymphoma Society
1311 Mamaroneck Ave.
White Plains, NY 10605
914-949-5213
www.leukemia.org

Pediatric AIDS Foundation
1311 Colorado Ave.
Santa Monica, CA 90405
310-395-9051

Shriners Hospitals for Children
c/o International Shrine
Headquarters
2900 Rocky Point Dr.
Tampa, FL 33607
813-281-0300
www.shrinershq.org

The Institute for Children with Cancer and Blood Disorders
P.O. Box 109
New Brunswick, NJ 08903
800-231-KIDS

The Smile Train
245 5th Ave., Ste. 2201
New York, NY 10016
877-KIDSMILE
212-689-9199
info@smiletrain.org

The Society for Pediatric Pathology
3643 Walton Way Extension
Augusta, GA 30909
706-364-3375
socpedpath@degnon.org
www.spponline.org

St. Jude Children's Research Hospital
National Executive Offices
501 St. Jude Pl.
Memphis, TN 38105
901-495-3300
lin.ballew@stjude.org
www.stjude.org

Sudden Infant Death Syndrome Alliance
1314 Bedford Ave., Ste. 210
Baltimore, MD 21208
800-221-SIDS
410-653-8709
info@sidsalliance.org

DEAF/HEARING IMPAIRED

American Tinnitus Association
P.O. Box 5
Portland, OR 97207-0005
800-634-8978
503-248-9985
tinnitus@ata.org

Deafness Research Foundation
1050 17th St., N.W., Ste. 701
Washington, DC 20036
202-289-5850
drf@drf.org
www.drf.org

DIABETES

American Diabetes Association
1701 N. Beauregard St.
Alexandria, VA 22311
800-342-2383
703-549-1500
membership@diabetes.org

Canadian Diabetes Association
(National Life Building)
1400-522 University Ave.
Toronto, ON M5G 2R5
Canada
800-226-8464
416-363-0177
info@diabetes.ca
www.diabetes.ca

City of Hope
1500 E. Duarte Rd.
Duarte, CA 91010
800-826-HOPE
626-359-8111

Joslin Diabetes Center
One Joslin Place
Boston, MA 02215
617-732-2400
www.joslin.harvard.edu

Juvenile Diabetes Foundation International
120 Wall St., 13th Fl.
New York, NY 10005
800-JDF-CURE
info@jrdf.org

177

DIGESTIVE DISORDERS

American Digestive Health Foundation
7910 Woodmont Ave.,
Ste. 700
Bethesda, MD 20814
301-654-2635

Crohn's and Colitis Foundation of America
386 Park Ave. S.,
17th Fl.
New York, NY 10016
info@ccfa.org

EYESIGHT

Foundation Fighting Blindness
(Formerly National
Retinitis Pigmentosa
Foundation)
11435 Cronhill Dr.
Owings Mills, MD 21117
888-394-3937
410-568-0150
info@blindness.org

Macular Degeneration Research
(a program of the
American Health
Assistance Foundation)
15825 Shady Grove Rd.,
Ste. 140
Rockville, MD 20850
800-437-AHAF
eberger@ahaf.org
www.ahaf.org

Massachusetts Lions Eye Research Fund
(formerly Lions Club
International Foundation)
118 Allen St.
Hampden, MA 01036
www.mlerf.com

National Glaucoma Research
(a program of the
American Health
Assistance Foundation)
15825 Shady Grove Rd.,
Ste. 140
Rockville, MD 20850
800-437-AHAF
eberger@ahaf.org
www.ahaf.org

Research to Prevent Blindness
645 Madison Ave., 21st Fl.
New York, NY 10022
800-621-0026
info@rpbusa.org

IMMUNE SYSTEM DISORDERS

Alliance for Lupus Research, Inc.
1270 Avenue of the
Americas, Ste. 609
New York, NY 10030
212-218-2840
www.lupusresearch.org

Lupus Foundation of America, Inc.
2000 L St., N.W.,
Ste. 710
Washington, DC 20036
800-558-0121
202-349-1155
202-349-1156
www.lupus.org

INHERITED ILLNESSES

Charcot-Marie-Tooth Association
2700 Chestnut St.
Chester, PA 19013-4867
800-606-CMTA
cmtassoc@aol.com
www.charcot-marie-tooth.org

Cystic Fibrosis Foundation
6931 Arlington Rd.
Bethesda, MD 20814
800-FIGHT-CF
301-951-4422
info@cff.org

Huntington's Disease Society of America
158 W. 29th St., 7th Fl.
New York, NY 10001
800-345-HDSA
212-239-3430
hdsainfo@hdsa.org

Osteogenesis Imperfecta Foundation, Inc.
804 West Diamond Ave.,
Ste. 210
Gaithersburg, MD 20878
800-981-2663
301-947-0456
www.oif.org

MENTAL ILLNESS

National Alliance for Research of Schizophrenia and Depression
60 Cutter Mill Rd.,
Ste. 404
Great Neck, NY 11021
800-829-8289
info@narsad.org
www.narsad.org

National Alliance on Mental Illness Research Institute
Colonial Place Three
2107 Wilson Blvd.,
Ste. 300
Arlington, VA 22201-3042
703-524-7600
www.nami.org

Tourettes Syndrome Association
42-40 Bell Blvd.
Bayside, NY 11361-2820
800-237-0717
718-224-2999
ts@tsa-usa.org
www.tsa-usa.org

MISCELLANEOUS

American Federation for Aging Research
70 W. 40th St., 11th Fl.
New York, NY 10018
212-703-9977
888-582-2327
amfedaging@aol.com

American Health Assistance Foundation
15825 Shady Grove Rd.,
Ste. 140
Rockville, MD 20850
800-437-AHAF
eberger@ahaf.org
www.ahaf.org

American Liver Foundation
75 Maiden Ln., Ste. 603
New York, NY 10038
800-465-4837
www.liverfoundation.org

American Lung Association
National Headquarters
1740 Broadway
New York, NY 10019
212-315-8700
info@lungusa.org

Arthritis Foundation
1330 W. Peachtree St.
Atlanta, GA 30309
404-872-7100

BNI Foundation
350 W. Thomas Rd.
Phoenix, AZ 85013
602-406-3041

**Endometriosis
Association**
8585 N. 76th Pl.
Milwaukee, WI 53223
800-992-3636
www.endometriosisassn.org

**Entertainment Industry
Foundation**
11132 Ventura Blvd.,
Ste. 401
Studio City, CA 91604
818-760-7722
www.eifoundation.org

**Life Extension
Foundation**
P.O. Box 229120
Hollywood, FL 33022
800-544-4440
www.lef.org

**National Jewish Medical
and Research Center**
1400 Jackson St.
Denver, CO 80206
303-388-4461
www.nationaljewish.org

**National Kidney
Foundation**
30 E. 33rd St., Ste. 1100
New York, NY 10016
800-622-9010
212-889-2210
info@kidney.org

**National Osteoporosis
Foundation**
1232 22nd St., N.W.
Washington, DC 20037
202-223-2226
bob@nof.org

**Plastic Surgery Education
Foundation**
(American Society of
Plastic & Reconstructive
Surgery (PSEF/ASPS))
444 E. Algonquin Rd.
Arlington Heights, IL
60005
847-228-9900

The Smile Train
245 5th Ave., Ste. 2201
New York, NY 10016
877-KIDSMILE
212-689-9199
info@smiletrain.org

**Stem Cell Research
Foundation**
22512 Gateway Center Dr.
Clarksburg, MD 20871
877-842-3442
www.stemcellresearchfoun-
dation.org

NEUROLOGICAL
DISORDERS

**Charcot-Marie-Tooth
Association**
2700 Chestnut St.
Chester, PA 19013-4867
800-606-CMTA
cmtassoc@aol.com
www.charcot-marie-
tooth.org

**Epilepsy Foundation
of America**
4351 Garden City Dr.,
Ste. 500
Landover, MD 20785
301-459-3700
info@efa.org

National Headache Foundation
428 W. St. James Pl.,
2nd Fl.
Chicago, IL 60614-2750
800-NHF-5552
773-525-7357
info@headaches.org

National Multiple Sclerosis Society
733 3rd Ave., 6th Fl.
New York, NY 10017
800-344-4867
infor@nmss.org

NEUROMUSCULAR DISORDERS

Amyotrophic Lateral Sclerosis Assn.
27001 Agoua Rd.,
Ste. 150
Calabasas Hills, CA
91301-5104
800-782-4747
818-880-9007
alsinfo@alsa-national.org

Families of Spinal Muscular Atrophy
P.O. Box 196
Libertyville, IL 60048
800-886-1762
847-367-7620
ama@fsma.org

Muscular Dystrophy Association
3300 E. Sunrise Dr.
Tucson, AZ 85718-3208
800-572-1717
mda@mdausa.org

Project ALS
511 Avenue of the
Americas
PMB #341
New York, NY 10011
800-603-0272
www.projectals.org

United Cerebral Palsy
1660 L St., N.W.,
Ste. 700
Washington, DC 20036
202-776-0406
ucpnatl@ucpa.org

PARALYSIS

American Paralysis Foundation
500 Morris Ave.
Springfield, NJ 07081
201-379-2690

The Buoniconti Fund
P.O. Box 016960, R-48
Miami, FL 33101
305-243-6001

Christopher Reeve Paralysis Foundation
500 Morris Ave.
Springfield, NJ 07081
800-225-0290
info@crpf.org

Eastern Paralyzed Veterans Association
75-20 Astoria Blvd.
Jackson Heights, NY
11370
718-803-3782
info@epva.org
www.unitedspinal.org

Miami Project to Cure Paralysis
P.O. Box 016960, R-48
Miami, FL 33101
800-STANDUP
305-243-6001
mpinfo@miamiproject.med.
miami.edu

Paralyzed Veterans of America
801 18th St., N.W.
Washington, DC 20006
800-424-8200
202-872-1300
info@pva.org

PARKINSON'S DISEASE

American Parkinson's Disease Assn.
1250 Hylan Blvd.,
Ste. 4B
Staten Island, NY 10305
800-223-2732
718-981-8001
info@apdaparkinson.com

The Michael J. Fox Foundation for Parkinson's Research
Grand Central Station
P.O. Box 4777
New York, NY 10163
800-708-7644

National Parkinson's Foundation
1501 N.W. 9th Ave.
Miami, FL 33136
800-327-4545
mailbox@parkinson.org

Parkinson's Disease Foundation, Inc.
710 W. 168th St.
New York, NY 10032
800-457-6676
212-923-4700
info@pdf.org

SKIN DISORDERS

National Psoriasis Foundation
6600 S.W. 92nd Ave.,
Ste. 300
Portland, OR 97223-7195
800-723-9166
503-244-7404
getinfo@npfusa.org

National Vitiligo Foundation, Inc.
611 S. Fleishel Ave.
Tyler, TX 75701
903-531-0074

VETERANS' HEALTH

Eastern Paralyzed Veterans Assn.
75-20 Astoria Blvd.
Jackson Heights, NY 11370
718-803-3782
info@epva.org
www.unitedspinal.org

Paralyzed Veterans of America
801 18th St., N.W.
Washington, DC 20006
800-424-8200
202-872-1300
info@pva.org

Do you see your favorite charity on this list?

You may wish to reconsider who receives your valuable support. But don't just stop making contributions – write to that organization and tell them, politely yet firmly, that they will not receive your support until they stop funding animal research.

Charities to contact:

FREQUENTLY ASKED QUESTIONS AND ANSWERS ABOUT ANIMAL TESTING

Why should I be concerned about animal testing?

The use of live animals to test everyday consumer products and their ingredients is a cruel and unnecessary practice. Millions of animals suffer and die each year in painful, distressing tests that produce only useless and irrelevant data.

Don't animal tests protect humans by determining product safety?

No. Animal tests do not ensure the safety of a product. Many products that are known to be hazardous, from oven cleaners to bleach, are readily available on store shelves with only a warning label and/or childproof cap. Moreover, no amount of animal testing can change the fact that many products are harmful if ingested or used in a way that's not intended by the manufacturer.

Aren't companies required by law to test their products on animals?

It depends on the type of product. The FDA, which administers the federal Food, Drug and Cosmetic Act, requires that pharmaceutical drugs, as well as products that are also intended to treat or prevent disease, or that affect the structure or functions of the human body (suntan lotions, antiperspirants, topical acne medications), must be tested on animals. But manufacturers of cosmetics are not required under federal regulations to conduct tests on animals.

Then why do these companies test on animals?

The FDA urges companies to conduct whatever toxicological tests are appropriate to substantiate the safety of their products. Traditionally, manufacturers have used animal tests to generate that substantiation. They also use animal tests as documentation of safety to help them in court in the event of a lawsuit.

Why do you say that animal testing is poor science?

Humans and nonhumans are different in many obvious and subtle ways; therefore, the results of animal tests cannot be reliably and accurately extrapolated from one species to another. Even the smallest biological difference among species can cause vastly different results. We must know first what happens in humans before we can make any determination if an animal can duplicate a human response. That is why we say that animal tests lack *predictability* and *relevance*.

What would we do if we didn't test on animals?

There are a wide range of scientifically valid non-animal methodologies that are available to safety-test products and ingredients. In addition to eliminating the suffering of animals, these methodologies have been shown to be more effective and cost-efficient.

How are these alternatives determined to be effective?

After a new alternative is developed, it must go through a rigorous validation process before it is considered reliable for general use. The Interagency Coordinating Committee on the Validation of Alternative Methods (ICCVAM), a permanent committee composed of representatives from 15 federal regulatory and research agencies, conducts reviews and hearings on alternatives.

ICCVAM was established to implement the directives of the National Institute of Environmental Health Sciences (NIEHS), which are to

"…establish, wherever feasible, guidelines, recommendations and regulations that promote the regulatory acceptance of new and revised toxicological tests that protect human and animal health and the environment while reducing, refining or replacing animal tests and ensuring human safety and productive effectiveness."

For more information on the non-animal alternatives that have been approved by ICCVAM, visit their website at www.ICCVAM.niehs.nih.gov.

What makes a product cruelty free?

The term "cruelty free" refers to the product testing policy of a company that does not use animals in testing either its ingredients or final products. However, a product listed as cruelty free in this book may contain ingredients that are derived from animal by-products. For a list of ingredients that are animal-derived, see page 154.

Why should I buy cruelty-free products?

If you are concerned about the suffering of animals in cruel and unnecessary tests, then buying products that have not been tested on animals is an important way to match your buying habits with your moral convictions.

Here's another good reason for selecting cruelty-free products: it sends a powerful message to companies that you won't support an industry that perpetuates animal suffering, while you do support companies that don't test on animals.

Why aren't there any store brands listed in Personal Care for People Who Care?

There are so many store brands and generic products on the market that space does not allow us to list them all. Also, many store brand products are manufactured by companies that produce the same national brands, but not always, and there are some companies that manufacture multiple store brands. Regrettably, NAVS does not have the resources to research every store brand that's available locally, regionally and nationally, especially considering the fact that many of these products come and go very quickly. We feel it is best to focus on "name" brands that are available across the country.

For more questions and answers on animal testing, please visit the FAQ section of our website at www.navs.org.

How can I be sure I'm purchasing a product that's truly cruelty free?

It's best to consult the main directory in this book for the best information that's available. That's because the information on product labels can be misleading. For example, if a label says "this product has not been tested on animals" it could mean that while the final product hasn't been animal-tested, the ingredients used in making it were animal-tested. Also, don't assume that a label that says "against animal testing" means that the product wasn't animal-tested.

I want to do my part to help end animal testing. What can I do?

There are many simple ways you can spread the word about animal testing and to make sure that *Personal Care for People Who Care* gets into the hands of as many people as possible. Turn to the next page and see!

Discovering

Making a Difference for Animals   190

About NAVS   192

NAVS Membership Application   195

More Ways to Help Animals

Making a Difference for Animals

Check out all the ways you can help end the cruelty and waste of animal testing.

Take *Personal Care for People Who Care* with you whenever you shop. That way, you'll never miss an opportunity to make the compassionate choice…and use the power of your pocketbook to make a strong statement to companies that continue to test their products on animals.

Give *Personal Care for People Who Care* as a gift. Your friends and family will appreciate the opportunity to learn more about cruelty-free shopping. And for anyone who wants to learn more about animal testing, this book provides the answers in a simple, easy-to-read format. You may order additional copies of *Personal Care for People Who Care* through our website at **www.navs.org**, or by calling us with your credit card at **800-888-NAVS** (800-888-6287).

Tell your local library, school or community center that they can contact us for a FREE copy of *Personal Care for People Who Care*. It's a great way to spread the word about animal testing and cruelty-free living throughout your community.

Voice your opposition to animal testing to companies that continue to test on animals. This is very important, because corporations are very concerned about their public image, and your polite but firm message, written from your heart, can have a powerful impact.

Contact your local newspapers and radio stations. Tell them you're concerned about how animals are treated in our society, and how animal testing causes grave suffering to animals while often harming humans. Have them contact NAVS and request our FREE radio public service announcements.

Contact your congressional representatives and let them know of your opposition to the exploitation of animals. Encourage them to support legislation that implements non-animal methods of ensuring public safety. If you don't know who your congressional representatives are or how to contact them, NAVS can help. Simply go to our website at **www.navs.org**. Or you can call us at **800-888-NAVS** (800-888-6287).

Become a NAVS partner by joining us in our struggle to spare animals from suffering. As a member of NAVS, you'll be informed about opportunities where you can truly make a difference for animals. And we'll keep you posted on news and developments regarding the issue of animal experimentation.

Turn to the next page and find out about all the ways NAVS works to save animal lives while building a future where every living creature will be treated with compassion, respect and justice. To join us in our efforts, simply complete and return the membership form on page 195. You may also join NAVS through our website at **www.navs.org**, where you can register for our timely e-newsletters and Action Alerts.

www.navs.org

About NAVS

We're working hard to spare animals from suffering while improving human health and safety.

As animal advocates for humane science, NAVS is dedicated to ending the cruelty and waste of animal experimentation on both ethical and scientific grounds. We believe that it is morally unacceptable to exploit one species for the benefit of another. There is also a huge body of evidence proving that animal testing lacks scientific credibility. NAVS seeks to promote more humane and effective ways to finding the answers we need to protect human health.

NAVS' programs are focused on education and advocacy. We believe that significant progress can be made by increasing the public's awareness that animal testing does not necessarily protect them, and may even put them at risk. We also seek to engage the scientific community as well as the legal and legislative arenas in our efforts, so that together we can effect positive change for animals and people.

Above all, our programs are designed to spare animal lives today while building a future where no animal is sacrificed under the false assumption that it helps people. These programs include:

The NAVS Dissection Alternatives Loan Program is the first and most extensive source for effective, state-of-the-art non-animal educational materials. These materials, which range from elementary through the post-graduate level, are available on a free-of-charge loan basis to students, teachers and school districts.

The NAVS Sanctuary Fund provides vital emergency assistance to animals in desperate need as a result of natural and human-made disasters. Through our Sanctuary Fund grants, we are able to provide the money necessary to finance a rescue effort without having to go through the time and expense of sending out an appeal to our members. In every case, the Fund's money is used to help ensure permanent, lifetime care for all the animals involved.

NAVS' funding of Americans For Medical Advancement (AFMA), a not-for-profit organization that promotes human wellness by exposing the lost opportunities for cures and the life-threatening results of animal-modeled biomedical research, helps to raise the profile of the scientific case against animal experimentation.

NAVS' funding of the International Foundation for Ethical Research (IFER), a not-for-profit organization that supports scientists who are developing non-animal testing methodologies, as well as post-graduate students who want to incorporate animal welfare into their studies and their future careers, helps promote more humane science.

3 easy ways to join NAVS!

1. Visit our website at **www.navs.org**.

2. Call us with your credit card at **800-888-NAVS** (800-888-6287).

3. Return the NAVS membership form on page 195.

Thank you for having a heart for animals!

NAVS' funding of the International Institute for Animal Law (IIAL), which is dedicated to providing attorneys and other legal advocates the resources they need to advance animal protection legislation, helps harness the power of the law to help animals.

We have made many strides for animals through these programs, but we still have a long way to go. Your support is critical to ensure that we will continue to be a voice for the innocent creatures who cannot speak for themselves.

NAVS MEMBERSHIP APPLICATION

Your support will make a real difference in our work to end animal suffering by helping us to continue our life-saving educational and advocacy programs. Call 800-888-NAVS or mail this application today to NAVS, 3701 Paysphere Circle, Chicago, IL 60674.

YES! I want to join the National Anti-Vivisection Society. I understand that my new membership includes one free copy of *Personal Care for People Who Care*, one free copy of NAVS' special publication *Expressions*, a year's subscription to the NAVS newsletter, *Animal Action Report* and frequent updates and action alerts throughout the year.

Please check all appropriate boxes below.

Annual Memberships

❏ Individual $25   PCN01
❏ Student $10   PCN06
❏ Senior $12   PCN05

Lifetime Memberships

❏ Life Sponsor $100   PCN04
❏ Life Benefactor $500   PCN02
❏ Life Partner $1,000   PCN03

❏ Please send additional information on NAVS' programs. PCG00
❏ I do not wish to join at this time, but please accept my donation of $_____. PCD10
❏ Please send me information on how I can enjoy the convenience of having a monthly donation debited from my credit card, checking or savings account. PCZ00
❏ My check is enclosed.
❏ Charge my   ❏ VISA   ❏ MasterCard   ❏ Discover   ❏ American Express

Account No. _____ Exp. Date _____

Signature _____

Telephone Number _____

Email Address _____

Name _____

Address _____

City _____ State_____ Zip_____

Please do not send cash. All contributions are tax-deductible to the fullest extent of the law. If you are using a credit card, you may also FAX this application to NAVS at 312-427-6524.